Mass Matters
WE ARE CALLED TO
GLORY

A Small Course on the Eucharistic Liturgy

By Rev. David B. Rosenberg

Rev. David Rosenberg

Mass Matters: A Small Course On The Holy Mass, the Sacrament Of The Eucharist

Unless otherwise indicated, Scripture quotations are from the New Revised Standard Version Bible, Catholic Edition, copyright 1989 by the Division of Christian Education of the National Council of Churches of Christ in the United States of America. Used by permission. All rights reserved.

Excerpts from the English translation of the Roman Missal © 2010, International Commission on English in the Liturgy Corporation, All Rights Reserved.

Copyright © 2022 Institute for Spiritual Direction; DeWitt, Michigan USA

http://www.isdministries.org/

Printed with Ecclesiastical Permission
Most Reverend Earl Boyea. October 9, 2022
Lansing, Michigan

All rights reserved. No part of this work may be reproduced in any form or by any means, electronic or mechanical, without the written permission of the publisher.

ISBN: 9798353954941
9/21/2022 on the Feast of St. Matthew

DEDICATION

This little book is dedicated to Dom. Gregory Hoppough, CSS,
spiritual father and liturgy professor
at Pope Saint John XXIII National Seminary in Weston Massachusetts;
in appreciation of a life dedicated to his Church, his daily inspirations,
and his profound love of the Eucharist
and the People of God.

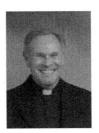

PHOTO BY THOMAS SHANNON

MASS MATTERS
We are called to glory

A SMALL COURSE ON THE EUCHARISTIC LITURGY

Table of Contents

ACKNOWLEDGMENTS

INTRODUCTION | 1

ENTRANCE RITES
LESSON 1 | Gathering For The Feast | 7

LITURGY OF THE WORD
LESSON 2 | Liturgy of the Word: Tell the Stories | 21

LESSON 3 | The Creed and Universal Prayer of the People | 37

LITURGY OF THE EUCHARIST, THE JOYFUL FEAST
LESSON 4 | The Barakah: Offering The Fruit Of The Earth And Work Of Human Hands | 45

LESSON 5 | The Preface : We are Called Together in His Name | 53

LESSON 6 | Eucharistic Prayers and Consecration: Preparing the Sacrificial Meal | 59

LESSON 7 | Anamnesis: Remembering our Past – Christ's Intercessions | 67

LESSON 8 | The Eucharistic Feast – Bread that is Broken and Shared | 73

CONCLUSION | A Transfiguration Experience | 81

ACKNOWLEDGMENTS

Special thanks to Cecelia Sheridan and Dr. Kevin Magas:
    Cecelia Sheridan was born in Pittsburgh, Pennsylvania in 1945. She completed her master's degree in European Philosophy at Duquesne University in Pittsburgh Pennsylvania in 1975, receiving the degree after a semester at Catholic University in Washington, D.C. in 1989. God blessed her with a career as a liturgist and adult religious director/pastoral associate for St. Andrew the Apostle Catholic Church in Saline. She retired in 2011.

    Dr. Kevin Magas, Ph.D. for theological and editorial assistance. Dr. Kevin serves as assistant professor in the department of dogmatic theology and director of intellectual formation for the Liturgical Institute University of Saint Mary of the Lake/Mundelein Seminary. He received his Master of Theological Studies degree and was a Ph.D. candidate in liturgical studies area of the Department of Theology at the University of Notre Dame at the time of the publishing of the first edition of Mass Matters. Dr Kevin specializes in sacramental and liturgical theology.

The author wishes to acknowledge the dedicated staff, students and alumni of the Institute for Spiritual Direction. As we present Mass Matters on retreats, at parish missions, and lecture series at parishes and retreat centers they are always there to form a team of pastoral professionals to be witnesses to the Eucharistic ethos that radiate joyfully from their hearts, minds and spirits. I am most grateful!

Fr David

Rev. David Rosenberg

Preface to the Second Edition

How Do We Learn To Pray And Live The Liturgy?

"I have eagerly desired to eat this Passover with you before I suffer" (Luke 22:15)

The Church in the United States began a three-year national Eucharistic Revival on June 19, 2022. One of the most important parts of the revival was aimed at helping to make the celebration of the Mass, the lived source, summit, and fountain of the life of the Church through all individual believers. For that to occur, the Church's theology of the liturgy must be assimilated, prayed and lived.

Vatican II began with a reflection on the liturgy. Pope St. Paul VI said during the Council, *"The liturgy is the first source of divine communion in which God shares His own life with us, the first school of the spiritual life, the first gift we must make to the Christian people."* Everything must begin with worshiping God. This assimilation process might well begin, then, with the source documents of Vatican II, "The Sacred Constitution of the Church." We do well to review paragraphs 14, 18 and 19:

> 14. Mother Church earnestly desires that all the faithful should be led to that *fully conscious and active participation in liturgical celebrations which is demanded by the very nature of the liturgy.* Such participation by the Christian people as "a chosen race, a royal priesthood, a holy nation, a redeemed people (1 Pet. 2:9; cf. 2:4-5), is *their right and duty by reason of their baptism.*
>
> In the restoration and promotion of the sacred liturgy, *this full and active participation by all the people is the aim to be considered before all else*; for it is the primary and indispensable source from which the faithful are to derive the true Christian spirit; and therefore pastors of souls must zealously strive to achieve it, by means of the necessary instruction, in all their pastoral work.
>
> Yet it would be futile to entertain any hopes of realizing this unless the pastors themselves, in the first place, become thoroughly imbued with the spirit and power of the liturgy, and undertake to give instruction about it. A prime need, therefore, is that attention be directed, first of all, to the liturgical instruction of the clergy. Wherefore the sacred Council has decided to enact as follows
>
> 18. Priests, both secular and religious, who are already working in the Lord's vineyard, are to be helped by every suitable means to understand ever more fully what it is that they are doing when they perform sacred rites; they are to be aided to live the liturgical life and to share it with the faithful

entrusted to their care.

> 19. With zeal and patience, pastors of souls must promote the liturgical instruction of the faithful, and also their active participation in the liturgy both internally and externally... By so doing, pastors will be fulfilling one of the chief duties of a faithful dispenser of the mysteries of God; and in this matter they must lead their flock not only in word but also by example.

Saint John Paul II, in his encyclical letter, *"Eucharistic Church"* promulgated April 17, 2003 wrote *"To contemplate Christ involves being able to recognize Him wherever He manifests himself, in His many forms of presence, but above all in the living sacrament of His body and His blood. The Church draws her life from Christ in the Eucharist; by Him she is fed and by Him she is enlightened. The Eucharist is both a mystery of faith and a "mystery of light".* Whenever the Church celebrates the Eucharist, the faithful can in some way relive the experience of the two disciples on the road to Emmaus: *"their eyes were opened and they recognized him" (Luke 24:31)."*

Fifteen years ago, in his apostolic exhortation *Sacramentum Caritatis (The Sacrament of Charity),* on the Eucharist as the Source and Summit of the Church's Life and Mission, Pope Benedict called for a *"mystagogical catechesis,"* a catechesis that initiates the faithful into the mystery of Christ, so that the faithful could *"make their interior dispositions correspond to their gestures and words."* Pope Benedict, in the letter, urges the faithful to live the liturgical reform promulgated at the Second Vatican Council. He prays that the Faithfull's full, active, conscious, fruitful and devout participation in the Mass might be fulfilled.

Pope Francis dedicated his 2022 Apostolic Letter *Desiderio Desideravi ("I longed for desire...")* to the liturgical formation of the people of God *"that all may be one in us." (John 17:23)* He speaks of Jesus' "burning" and "infinite" yearning to bring everyone into communion with Him through eating His body and drinking His blood. Pope Francis points out that at the beginning of the Last Supper, Jesus told the apostles, *"I have eagerly desired to eat this Passover with you before I suffer" (Luke 22:15)* and that desire, the Pope says, precedes our attendance at Mass and every pious reception of him.

Pope Francis calls on the Church to work *"so that all can be seated at the Supper of the sacrifice of the Lamb and live through Him, with Him and from Him."* He urges us not to *"allow ourselves even a moment of rest, knowing that still not everyone has received an invitation to this Supper or that others have forgotten it or have got lost along the way in the twists and turns of human living."*

The problem today is that many people attend Mass without

consciously encountering Christ, without an awareness of what is taking place. That is why, he says, there are inestimable benefits gained from the Church's getting the liturgy right and forming others to appreciate it, enter into it and live it.

"Is this not the same movement as the Paschal meal of the risen Jesus with his disciples? Walking with them he explained the Scriptures to them; sitting with them at table 'he took bread, blessed and broke it, and gave it to them.'" (CCC 1347)

INTRODUCTION

Gather the folks, tell the stories, break the bread.

The liturgy of the holy Mass[1] is our Eucharistic feast, a gift given to us by Jesus.

"Liturgy" is defined as the *"public prayer of the Church."* The Mass is our *"public prayer"* that feeds the soul and strengthens us for the journey to *"…go and make disciples of all nations."(Mt 28:19)*

The fundamental structure of the Mass has been preserved throughout the centuries down to our own day. It is the structure where Jesus gathered the folks in the encounter of two disciples on the road to Emmaus as recorded in Luke's Gospel. Jesus then told the stories, reflecting on Scripture, revealing the purpose and necessity of His Passion. (Luke 24: 25-27) He then revealed himself raised from the dead, took bread, said the blessing, broke it, and gave it to them. (Luke 24: 29-31)

Tell the story and share the sacred feast:
Liturgy of the Word and Liturgy of the Eucharist

These two parts, the Liturgy of the Word and Liturgy of the Eucharist, are the ancient and contemporary shape of the Mass; two parts that together form "one single act of worship."[2] The Eucharistic table prepared for us is the table both of the Word of God and of the body of the Lord. The Church is nourished spiritually at this twofold table – from the one it

---

[1] CCC 1332 Holy Mass ("Missa"), because the liturgy in which the mystery of salvation is accomplished concludes with the sending forth ("missio") of the faithful, so that they may fulfill God's will in their daily lives.

[2] CCC 1346 The Liturgy of the Eucharist unfolds according to a fundamental structure, which has been preserved throughout the centuries down to our own day. It displays two great parts that form a fundamental unity: The gathering, the Liturgy of the Word, with readings, homily and general intercessions and the Liturgy of the Eucharist, with the presentation of the bread and wine, the consecratory thanksgiving and Communion. The Liturgy of the Word and Liturgy of the Eucharist together form "one single act of worship"; the Eucharistic table set for us is the table both of the Word of God and of the body of the Lord.

grows in wisdom and from the other in holiness.[3]

Although the parts have formal names, the shape of the Mass is actually rather simple. It includes all the elements of a feast – good company, songs, stories and food. Jesus is the host and all present have been called. This feast circles the globe, bridges space and time and includes the most diverse collection of souls. It's the kind of feast where all are encouraged to participate in the preparations and help the host bring the sacrificial feast to the table.

> *"The whole community thus joins in the unending praise that the Church in heaven, the angels and all the saints, sing to the thrice-holy God." (CCC 1352)*

The Mass, of course, is more than a feast. It is a celebration where creator and creation meet in a loving mystical embrace. The Liturgy of the Word and Liturgy of the Eucharist together form this single act of worship. Liturgy is not a reenactment of the Last Supper as a mere historical event – it is the incarnation of Jesus Christ.

The "Word" is still becoming flesh and lives among us. The Eucharist is God's real physical presence in the world. The Eucharist is the place where Jesus continues to take on physical flesh just as He once did in the womb of Mary.

One of the most enigmatic terms that Christians use to celebrate and think about their faith is the word *mystery*. It is best to try to understand it from a historical perspective.

From the time of the apostles, the Christian community celebrated the rites of Baptism and Eucharist in obedience to the Lord's commands (Matthew 28:19; Luke 22:19). From as early as the second century, these rites were referred to as *mysteries*. A deep intuition and insight is carried in this word as it relates to those ritual practices. Saint Paul in his theology used the word *mystery* as a key concept of what had happened in Christ. For Saint Paul the central *mystery* is the Cross of Christ. He renders in a single word the concept that something was hidden in the Cross that cannot be understood without being revealed. As He explains in the second chapter of the first letter to the Corinthians, when "the rulers of this age" crucified Christ, they did not understand who He was, for His true identity was hidden.

---

[3] "General Introduction to the Lectionary" (Second Edition); paragraph 10: "The Essential Bond between the Word of God and the Mystery of the Eucharist."

But in fact the rulers of that age crucified "the Lord of Glory." This is because, *"None of the rulers of this age knew this wisdom, because if they had known it, they would not have crucified the Lord of glory." (1 Corinthians 2:8).*

For Saint Paul it is not only the Lord of Glory that is hidden in the cross of Christ. So much unfolds from the cross, which to all appearances is but the ignominious death of a criminal. In fact, the entire plan of God for the world is hidden in the cross:

"In reading this, then, you will be able to understand my insight into the mystery of Christ, which was not made known to people in other generations as it has now been revealed by the Spirit to God's holy apostles and prophets. This mystery is that through the gospel the Gentiles are heirs together with Israel, members together of one body, and sharers together in the promise in Christ Jesus." (Ephesians 3:4-6).

The phrase *"mystery of the Eucharist"* means that the Eucharist is bread but within it a divine reality is hidden – an outward sign of an interior, hidden grace. The word in the singular, "*mystery of the Eucharist*," refers to the rite as a whole. The Eucharist is also called *"the mysteries"* expressing the various dimensions that work together. Gestures, words, bread and wine, the baptized faithful assembled in their various roles are all mysteries. In them is hidden the Lord of Glory. The Presider recalls this at the beginning of the Mass as he urges the congregation, *"As we prepare to celebrate these sacred mysteries, let us call to mind our failings and our sins."* And later, in the Eucharistic Prayer, the Presider announces, *"The mystery of faith,"* and the assembled baptized faithful cry out what is hidden in the consecrated bread and wine, the mystery that by His Cross and Resurrection, He has set us free.

The mysteries are events from the life of Christ in which divine realities are hidden. The word also refers to the central precept of Christian faith: the mystery of the Holy Trinity. This means that within the incarnate life of Jesus is hidden and now revealed the one God: Father, Son, and Holy Spirit. The life of Jesus, up to His Death, is called the Paschal Mystery, meaning that from the paschal sacrifice of His Death the Resurrection, the Ascension, the sending of the Spirit, and the Church unfolds. The word *mystery* preserves the tension between the physical and the divine. What is present exceeds and overflows the limits of the mere physical elements, even if the mystery is present only by means of it. This is mysterious in a way unique to Christian understanding. These are imponderable mysteries, yet through Christ there beckons a deeper entry into it and a path to live and move and have our beings within it. In the Roman Rite the word *"sacrament"* and *"mystery"* are synonymous, coming from the Latin *sacramentum* and *mysterion*.

Rev. David Rosenberg

In the first four or five centuries of the Church there was an instinctive sense of the nature of a sacrament. The bread and wine was a sacrament of the Lord's Body and Blood. By means of bread and wine we come into contact with something that now would otherwise be beyond reach. The nexus and core event in the entire history of humankind, the salvation of the world through the risen and glorified Body of Christ, is no longer confined to space and time. By means of a sacrament we come into contact in space and time with something that transcends space and time. The sacrament is the enfleshment of the transcendent body of the Lord. With Christ in this enfleshment we partake of the sacrament of His Body and thereby make contact with His Body through our body. The sacramental experience is at one and the same time physical and transcendent, just as Christ is present within physical reality and transcendent. It took several centuries to establish the view that the Eucharist is both real without being crudely realistic, and symbolic without being unreal.

To delve into the meaning of the Mass, first consider the bread and the wine. Then the movements of the people that become imbued and enmeshed with divine life itself. This is the sacramental perspective. The material matter of bread and wine are not "merely" or "weakly" symbolic. They are at one and the same time physically present and transcendent.

The songs we sing at Mass laud the host and His guests, the story and the sacramental feast. You are invited to join with this great gathering so that your spirit will be lifted up. This series of lessons is an attempt to help you see the liturgy with new senses so that eyes that have not seen will see, ears that have not heard will hear, and the mouth that has been silent might proclaim the meaning and purpose of this prayer to the glory of God.

Rev. David Rosenberg

ENTRANCE RITE

LESSON 1

Gathering for the Feast

Called to assemble we all gather together; we greet and prepare for the sacred feast, a memorial of His death and resurrection

The procession: From your house to Christ's "House of Many" and from sacristy to altar.

In the spring of 57 A.D., twenty-four years after the death and resurrection of Jesus, an assembly of followers of the *"Way"* gathered in Troas. They assembled as a memorial of the death and resurrection of Jesus, a sacrament of love, a sign of unity, a bond of charity, a Paschal feast through the breaking of the bread and the passing of the cup. They began their gathering listening to the Apostle Paul,[4] reminding them that the celebration of the Mass was the source and summit of all life[5] to do in remembrance. (1 Cor 11:23-26) We, too, gather together on the first day of the week for the breaking of bread where the body of Christ is consumed, the heart and mind is filled with grace, and a pledge of future glory is given. To come together, we travel from our homes, arrive and enter a building. As we fill the space, we begin to assemble the holy Church of Christ in that place.

The word *"church"* is used to translate a Greek word: *"ekklēsia,"* "the

---

[4] CCC 1323 "At the Last Supper, on the night He was betrayed, our Savior instituted the Eucharistic sacrifice of his body and blood. This He did in order to perpetuate the sacrifice of the cross throughout the ages until He should come again, and so to entrust to his beloved Spouse, the Church, a memorial of his death and resurrection: a sacrament of love, a sign of unity, a bond of charity, a Paschal banquet 'in which Christ is consumed, the mind is filled with grace, and a pledge of future glory is given to us.'"

[5] CCC 1324 The Eucharist is "the source and summit of the Christian life." "The other sacraments, and indeed all ecclesiastical ministries and works of the apostolate, are bound up with the Eucharist and are oriented toward it. For in the blessed Eucharist is contained the whole spiritual good of the Church, namely Christ himself, our Pasch."

called out assembly:"[6]

> *"And we know that in all things God works for the good of those who love him, who have been called according to his purpose. For those God foreknew he also predestined to be conformed to the image of his Son, that he might be the firstborn among many brothers and sisters. And those he predestined, he also called; those he called, he also justified; those he justified, he also glorified."* Romans 8:28-30

The called assembly is used to translate a Hebrew word: *"quahal."* The composition of *"quahal"* is first defined in the book of Nehemiah:

> *"The assembly, which consisted of men, women and children old enough to understand."* (Nehemiah 8:2)

ENTRANCE CHANT

Christ is coming and standing in the midst of His people

After the people have gathered, the Entrance chant begins as the priest enters with the deacon and ministers.[7] The purpose of this chant is to open the celebration, foster the unity of those who have been gathered, introduce their thoughts to the mystery of the liturgical season or festivity, and accompany the procession of the priest and ministers. It bespeaks the beauty of the one faith in the many Christians throughout the world. Song expresses the unity of the faith of the assembly in its various parts. Many voices together make one beautiful sound, a symphony. In song all the different qualities of voices and expression blend into one beautiful sound and one beautiful voice. This is the voice of the Church. It is a sounding, an incarnation of the unity of faith, of intercession, of praise from the one Church poised to celebrate the one Eucharist.

While the processional is being sung, various ministers of the liturgy moves through the church and into the sanctuary. At the culminating point of this procession is the Presider, rendering visible and for us what our eyes cannot see; Christ himself as the head of our assembly and the one who

---

[6] CCC 1348 All gather together. Christians come together in one place for the Eucharistic assembly where the Eucharist is celebrated amid the assembly of the faithful, the visible expression of the Church. All have their own active parts to play in the celebration, each in his own way: readers, those who bring up the offerings, those who give Communion and the whole people whose "Amen" manifests their participation.

[7] G.I.R.M. 46-47 Entrance Chant

leads us in prayer. This procession acts out and actually causes to happen what it signifies. Christ is coming and standing in the midst of His people.

Other ministers accompany the Presider in the procession, all dressed in special and different vestments signifying the difference in their roles. Some carry candles, another carries the smoking incense. But the liturgy is always more than the sum of its parts. When candles and incense enter, the heavenly choirs of angels enter the sanctuary with them; and they will help us to worship. They will pray for us and with us. They will protect us because they love us. In the procession the Deacon of the Word carries the Book of the Gospels. This shows us that Christ is coming together with His word. In what is about to happen, He will speak words of power and wisdom, a transforming word that will change our lives and form us into the likeness of himself. The Book of the Gospels will be placed on the altar in the same place where the holy gifts of bread and wine will later appear. So we see from the start the inseparability of the food of the Word and the food of the Lord's Body and Blood. We see that all the scriptures culminate in the sacrifice that will lie on the altar.

While the assembly is still singing, the Presider circles the altar with incense as a sign of reverencing the holy table around which, and on which all that is about to happen is concentrated. The sight of the incense and the mysterious atmosphere it creates, its sweet and unusual smell, as well as the glad song that still continues as we take the measure of the place where we now stand and the event that is about to happen. The altar is nothing less than the throne of God and of the Lamb.

The human capacity to sing is truly wonderful. Human song is an image of the mystery of the Incarnation. Air in a body, in a throat, pushing the intelligible voice outward in beautiful expression is an image of Spirit in the flesh, of divinity joined to humanity. It is magnificent and well expressive of our emotion. The beauty of our assembly, the beauty of our emotion, comes from Christ who has joined His divinity to our flesh so that He may lead His body in the song of thanksgiving to His Father. Rightly did Saint Augustine exclaim, *"To sing is to pray twice."*

Much has gone into the preparation for this Mass, and the actual beginning of the liturgical ceremony is a culmination of many graces mysteriously at work in the lives of hundreds and even thousands of people. Mass begins with the creation of the world. God intended this kind of encounter with His creatures from the start. The creation of the world and the history of the human race is the largest context for Mass, and this context is in fact presupposed and expressed in many of the rituals and texts. There is deep theological significance hidden in the arrival of many people coming from many places into one place to celebrate the Eucharist as the mystery of the assembly. The Mass begins as this called assembly forms. Within this mystery the assembly rejoices. In the coming together of many people into one place to be led and publicly pray with the Presider, we bring to reality profoundly what Church is called to be.

The baptized faithful in this assembly is in itself a sacred mystery hidden in their coming. Within the purpose driven life of every one of the baptized who has come to celebrate, the Eucharist stands as a magnificent personal story of grace, of struggle and labor and rejoicing. All have received their faith through others who have believed before them and have passed it on. This is Church, and the passing on of faith has this celebration as its ultimate point of arrival. From the four corners of creation, faith brings many believers together into one place. This gathering of many people into one place has a specific scope. They are disposed toward undergoing a divine action. The many will be made one, not through some means of their own devising but by receiving from Christ himself that life which He receives from another, from His eternal Father. It is by receiving from the Lord themselves these many who are gathered are brought into a unity which has divine origins. The name for this unity is Church, the assembly of those whom God has called out.

In this Eucharistic liturgy, many elements express one complex reality that is occurring; indeed, these elements embody and ensure the particular and precise nature of what is happening; namely, that Christ is acting and that the community is entirely defined and comes into being only through what He does and accomplishes. It is the Presider acting as the Head of the Person of Christ leads this assembly to glory. Christ gathers us; under His authority the Presider stands; it is Christ's word that is heard and pondered; it is together with him that the community will dare to speak a word back to the Father and make its thanksgiving offering to Him.

All this happens in a particular time and place. That time and place are also significant for understanding the mystery of the Church, for in the Eucharist the one time and place of a particular gathering, existing in a specific culture and in a precise moment in history with all the life stories of those who have come together, are expansively made to contain in this particular form the mystery of the universal Church across the world and across the centuries and across the heavens extending to the community of saints and angels in heaven. In any one gathering of a community to celebrate Eucharist, this whole reality of Church is expressed in the signs of the liturgy and is brought into being. For it to come to be, Church must be local and located in time. But the local church is more than the sum of its parts. The local church is an icon of the universal Church. In the Eucharistic Prayer the local bishop is named, as is the bishop of Rome, with whom the local bishop and bishops across the world verify their communion and apostolic faith. The saints in heaven are named, and the dead are remembered. The year of the celebration is recorded on the Easter candle, first lit with the first of the Easter Vigil celebration. All in the language and cultural traditions of the particular place. Called to this particular liturgy is hidden in the mystery of this assembly a much bigger assembly. The Church in heaven and on earth in that Church is the Mystical Body of Christ and the desire of every human heart. The Mass that is about to begin has been prepared by Our Father at the at the dawning creation. The meaning of the whole creation and the whole of human history is contained here, in ritual form and in the people who enact the ritual. This action will cause the Church to be. To celebrate this Eucharistic Liturgy is to be Church. To be Church, to be assembled into one, is what God intends for the world. The Eucharist is celebrated in thanksgiving and for the glory of God, and it is done for the salvation of the whole world.[8]

As we, men, women and children settle into our places, our procession is completed by the entrance in procession of the Presider, one or two deacons and servers. We stand at attention. When the Presider arrives at the altar, the sign of Christ's sacrifice, he kisses it and turns to us saying, *"Peace be with you."*[9] Our answer is, *"And with your spirit."* At that moment, in this place, peace is promised and the gathering of Church complete.

These words are not the words of any common social gathering. This is an exchange uniquely belonging to the Christian community and peculiar to this moment in the community's life when it begins to celebrate the source and summit of its life. The priest greets the people in his sacramental role of representing Christ at the head of His body, as Christ who will lead His body in prayer. And he speaks to the people, recognizing in them the assembly that God has called together. He sees them as an assembly of baptized people who are poised for the great sacrifice and act of worship to which their Baptism has admitted them. He spreads his arms wide as he

---

[8] Cf What Happens At Mass, by Jeremy Driscoll, OSB; Liturgy Training Publications (c) 2005, 2011

[9] CCC 2302 By recalling the commandment, "You shall not kill," our Lord asked for peace of heart ... Anger is a desire for revenge. "...it is praiseworthy to impose restitution to correct vices and maintain justice." The Lord says, "Everyone who is angry with his brother shall be liable to judgment."

speaks in a stylized gesture of gracious openness. It is the Lord himself whom we are meant to see and hear, spoken in profound words.

These words come from greetings which the apostle Paul used in his letters. The full and living Gospel has been preserved in the Church the apostles left to bishops as their successors in *"apostolic succession."*[10] The ordained priest is *"in the person of Christ the head,"* *"in persona Christi Capitis"*[11] as the head of His community. In this way, Christ passed on His mission and authority before being taken from their sight. The liturgy is meant to express all this as the bishops share their apostolic ministry of leadership with priests in the greetings. With this greeting we are reminded that the faith in which we stand comes to us from the apostles. Immediately we feel our community with them and with the saints who through generations of faithfulness have carried the apostolic faith to our times. With one of these formulas the priest is addressing the people with a greeting from God Himself, coming to us through Christ Jesus. It is a way of immediately lifting the assembly up.

The Presider's greeting to the people is on an exalted level, and the people's response must be no less highly pitched. They answer, "*And with your spirit.*" This response, is a formulation from the earliest centuries, is meant to be understood as the people addressing the *"spirit"* of the priest; that is, that deepest interior part of His being where He has been ordained precisely to lead the people in this sacred action. They are saying in effect, *"Be the priest for us now,"* aware that there is only one priest, Christ himself, and that this one who represents Him now is present to perform His sacred duties well.

Only in the tones that dignify this occasion between priest and people can we begin this liturgy, for the exchange expresses and establishes the unique harmony between ourselves, our Presider, and the Church throughout the world, which holds the faith that comes to us from the

---

[10] CCC 77 "In order that the full and living Gospel might always be preserved in the Church the apostles left bishops as their successors. They gave them their own position of teaching authority." Indeed, "the apostolic preaching, which is expressed in a special way in the inspired books, was to be preserved in a continuous line of succession until the end of time."

[11] A priest is *in persona Christi* as he acts as Christ and as God. An extended term, *in persona Christi capitis,* "in the person of Christ the head," was introduced at the Vatican Council II in the Decree on the Ministry and Live of Priests, Presbyterorum Ordinis, December 7, 1965.

apostles.

THE SIGN OF THE CROSS

After the hymn is ended and all are gathered in their places, the Presider invokes the Sign of the Cross[12], signing his body with the cross and saying the words *"In the name of the Father, and of the Son, and of the Holy Spirit."* All the people likewise sign themselves and answer, *"Amen."* The sign expresses in one summary gesture the central event of Christian faith. We trace it over our own bodies as a way of indicating that that event shall make its force felt on our very bodies. The Body that was crucified on the Cross touches us and shapes us for what is about to happen. In this signing, the mystery of the Holy Trinity is revealed in the Death of Jesus on the Cross. As the Mass proceeds, details will unfold for all to experience. Our bodies will be drawn into the Body that hung on the Cross, and this sharing in the Death of Christ is the revelation of the Trinitarian mystery.

The origin of the sign of the cross comes from the risen Lord himself who commanded His disciples to make disciples of all the nations, baptizing them *"in the name of the Father, and of the Son, and of the Holy Spirit."* He then makes a promise we can carry in confidence for the rest of our lives, *"And know that I am with you always, until the end of the world"* (Matthew 28:19-20).

In baptism we are plunged into the name of God in the living waters of the River of Life, flowing from the side of Christ into the baptismal font of every church. It is a mystery, yet as sacrament it is visible in our life. By means of it we are initiated into the very life of God, and this life is Father, Son, and Holy Spirit, a Father who begets a Son, a Son who yields utterly to the Father, and a Spirit who from their love proceeds. Baptism is also the sacramental immersion into the Death and Resurrection of Christ. To go down into the water is the mystery of dying and being buried with Him. To come up from the water is the mystery of rising with Him. In this gesture we signify the Cross and the Trinitarian name of God. The rest of the Christian life is a living out of the consequences of the baptism and an ever deepening entry into this divine mystery. Every time we mark the sign of the cross on our bodies and pronounce at the same time the holy name of

---

[12] CCC 2157 The Christian begins his day, his prayers, and his activities with the Sign of the Cross: "in the name of the Father and of the Son and of the Holy Spirit. Amen." The baptized person dedicates the day to the glory of God and calls on the Savior's grace which lets him act in the Spirit as a child of the Father. The sign of the cross strengthens us in temptations and difficulties.

God the Father, Son, and Holy Spirit we are reminding ourselves of the River of Life flowing from the side of Christ on the cross, a gift for our Baptism, a gift for the taking throughout in our lives.

The sign of the cross at the beginning of Mass, then, is the door through which we enter the Eucharistic mystery as we recall our own death at our baptism, joined with Christ in His Death and Resurrection. What we are about to experience is a deepening of what was begun in us at Baptism. In this moment is nothing less than Christian Baptism brought to its fullest pitch.

THE PENITENTIAL RITE

Conflict is a human condition. The first task in forming a community of human persons is making peace. This opening ritual is essential to the creation of a worshiping assembly of mutually caring human beings. It is a mutual announcement that in this place peace is willed and established.

For all human festal assemblies, we first prepare ourselves. Think of the festal family meals of Thanksgiving or Christmas. Those who prepare the feast and those who gather to consume it dress for the feast and wash their hands prior to preparing and consuming it. But there is something deeper that goes on as well. We consider the health of our relationships with whom we will gather. This, too, calls to mind our need for mutual forgiveness through spiritual cleansing and healing.

The worshiping assembly prepares itself by asking God for a pure heart and praying to have sins washed away through a penitential ritual. There are four possible penitential prayers that can be used for Mass. Three of them are dialogue prayers and one is a mutual prayer of priest and people.

Penitential Act, Form A (Confiteor)

"I confess to almighty God and to you, my brothers and sisters,
that I have greatly sinned in my thoughts and in my words,
in what I have done and in what I have failed to do,
through my fault, through my fault, through my most grievous fault; therefore I ask
blessed Mary ever-Virgin, all the angels and saints, and you, my brothers and sisters, to
pray for me to the Lord our God."

All four Penitential Acts are completed by the Presider's prayer of petition for God's forgiveness, to which the assembly responds *"Amen."*

"*Amen*," the Hebrew word meaning "So be it" or "It is the truth" is the oldest prayer of the Christian community. As a Hebrew word, it comes from our ancestors in faith, the first century Jewish communities of Palestine who heard and accepted Jesus of Nazareth, the Messiah of God. It is a one word statement of agreement, acceptance and commitment made by a free people. We and that first century assembly in Troas say together "Amen" to the One who calls us into relationship.

THE GLORIA

With the Gloria we come to the first element in the Mass that is not always a part of every celebration. The Gloria is sung on Sundays and the feasts, though not on the Sundays of Advent and Lent. (In Advent and Lent we abstain from singing this hymn so that it can ring out with fresh vigor on the feasts for which these seasons prepare us.)

The "Gloria" that we sing or recite at Mass echoes that angelic hymn, the song of the angels who surround the throne of God. *"The Church, in the Gloria, has extended this song of praise, which the angels sang in response to the event of the holy night, into a hymn of joy at God's glory – 'we praise you for your glory.'"* (Pope Benedict Homily at Midnight Mass, Christmas, 2010) In the "Gloria," we voice a joy that cannot be contained at the goodness of God now visible and tangible in the birth of Christ and in His saving work as our redeemer.

*"Glory to God in the highest,
and on earth peace to people of good will.
We praise you, we bless you, we adore you, we glorify you,
we give you thanks for your great glory, Lord God, heavenly King,
O God, almighty Father.
Lord Jesus Christ, Only Begotten Son,
Lord God, Lamb of God,
Son of the Father,
you take away the sins of the world,
have mercy on us;
you take away the sins of the world, receive our prayer;
you are seated at the right hand of the Father, have mercy on us.
For you alone are the Holy One,
you alone are the Lord,
you alone are the Most High, Jesus Christ, with the Holy Spirit,
in the glory of God the Father. Amen."*

By using the angels' same words we know that we are singing with them now, or we could just as well say it in the other direction: they are singing with us. We are singing now for the same reason that the angels first sang;

namely, that God has sent His Son among us born in our same flesh. Humble and lowly He comes among us, and so, struck with awe at this unexpected shape of the divine plan, as the angels themselves were, we cry out in a hymn to God's glory.

This hymn, on the days when it is sung, is an outburst of joy and praise. The liturgy is on the verge of beginning its first major part in the Liturgy of the Word, but it is as if we can hardly get started because of the joy and wonder of Sunday or the feast. So we stand and sing this hymn in anticipation of God wanting to address us in His word. We glorify God in the name of the Father and the Son who is seated at His right hand.

When the "Gloria" is concluded, the Presider with hands joined says: *"Let us pray."* And all pray in moment of silence with the Presider. Then the Presider with hands extended says the *"Collect"*[13] prayer at the end of which the assembly acclaims: *"Amen."*

THE OVERARCHING SHAPE OF THE ENTIRE RITE

The shape of the Entrance Rite has two basic movements coalescing as one which defines its essential form. The first is a movement from God the Father to the world, while the second is a movement from the world to God the Father. At any given point in the rite we will want to understand in which of these two directions the words and actions are moving. However, these two directions unfold in both a Trinitarian and an ecclesial shape that needs to be understood in order to sense in wonder and awe the fullest resonance of what is moving.

The first movement in this full Trinitarian and ecclesial shape can be described as follows: the Father gives Himself through the Son in the Holy Spirit, piercing the heavens with a circular spiritual wind that settles down upon and animates those assembled. Take a moment to ponder the depth and mystery of what this means. Without the wisdom and holiness that illuminates us to this dimension of the Eucharist, such Trinitarian formulations are perhaps just pious and habitually uttered phrases. Yet what we are dealing with here is the form, the dynamic, the very shape of God's

---

[13] "General Instruction of the Roman Missal" (GIRM) #54 Collect: The priest calls upon the people to pray and everybody, together with the priest, observes a brief silence so that they may become aware of being in God's presence and may "call to mind their intentions." Through the Collect "the character of the celebration finds expression." By an ancient tradition of the Church, the Collect prayer is usually addressed to God the Father, through Christ, in the Holy Spirit.

saving activity on our behalf; namely, that God the Father gives Himself to the world by giving His Son. This is *"the Father who so loved the world that He gave His only Son"* (John 3:16). But there is more. This direction of movement in the liturgy reveals that the Father gives His Son in and by the Holy Spirit who is Spirit of the Father. The Father gives His Spirit to illuminate, clarify and arrange everything in such a way that the Son be known and that all who believes in Him might live their lives entirely from the Son's life. It is this precise Trinitarian form that is revealed in what happens at Mass; the Father gives Himself to the world in the giving of His Son, a Son at every moment accompanied by the action and work of the Holy Spirit.

The second part is this shape of the divine mercy of God: the Church herself: the actual gathered assembly to whom the Father's Son is actually given. It is through the Church that the Father gives His Son to the world. The Church then celebrates Eucharist knowing that her mission is to bring everyone and indeed everything to the Eucharistic table as a gift to be presented for transformation. This is the mission of the Church because "*this being brought to the altar*" is what has been revealed as the will of the Father for all.

"God wants all to be saved and to come to know the truth." Timothy 2:5.

The community that celebrates Eucharist knows precisely from the celebration itself that all matter and all history have received in Christ a future which is nothing less than a share in His victory over sin and death. Everything and everybody in the world is destined by grace for Eucharistic transformation. The Father gives His Son to the world through the Church.

In this circular fashion of a "holy wind" the world gives back to the Father the grace she has received. In the first movement the Father places His Son into the hands of the Church. He does so in order that the Church, in the second movement, may offer what was given back to the Father. The Church exists not for herself but for the sake of the world. Only as we name Father, Son, and Spirit in describing this twofold movement of the Eucharistic liturgy, we acknowledge in humble adoration that it is not possible to do so without Our Lord first creating the Church for the world.

COLLECT

Our gathering is no accident and our assembly as Church is filled with purpose: We the baptized are called by God to gather. Our purpose is to celebrate an event that happened in the past, continues in the present and is made present in the moment by the prayer of priest and people. Because we have gathered for this celebration, a memorial sacrificial feast, we prepare ourselves for our communal prayer by reflecting on our trespasses and asking each other and the entire Church to pray that forgiven by God's grace we may honestly join in the pouring out of our cup of suffering in oblation into the Cup of Salvation of Jesus Christ. With hearts now made pure by God's grace, we cry out "Gloria" in joy and praise Him who is the host of the feast. Briefly, the Presider gathers all the needs and hopes of this assembly and offers them in prayer to God. In his opening prayer, the "Collect,"[14] the character and shape of the celebration finds expression. This completes the entrance rites of the Mass. He takes his seat and we follow his example.

The term "Collect" is the opening prayer that helps us to understand well this moment. It effectively places us all together into one succinctly expressed address to God the Father.

The prayer is addressed to Him and is always structured according to the same pattern, according to a very ancient usage. It helps to be attentive and listen for this pattern. God is first addressed in one or more of His many titles, thus, *"Almighty ever-living God."* Next we remember before God what God has done, certainly not because He has forgotten, but because *remembering is from biblical times a fundamental form of prayer.* On the basis of what is remembered, we ask for something in the present, for ourselves and for the whole Church and world, which is assembled in our assembling. When we remember what God has done in the past, we have courage and reason to hope for what we ask for in the present. If it is a feast, what we remember before God in the prayer is the particular saving event that is the subject of the feast. Something similar is awakened in the liturgical seasons. On Sundays in Ordinary Time, some more generally formulated saving action of God is recalled, but it is always an event remembered that becomes the basis for petition.

In the pattern of the Collect, we have the shape or pattern of prayer that will mark all the praying of the Mass. All the prayers are addressed to God

---

[14] "General Instruction of the Roman Missal" (GIRM) #54 Collect: The priest calls upon the people to pray and everybody, together with the priest, observes a brief silence so that they may become aware of being in God's presence and may "call to mind their intentions." Through the Collect "the character of the celebration finds expression." By an ancient tradition of the Church, the Collect prayer is usually addressed to God the Father, through Christ, in the Holy Spirit …

the Father, through the Son, in the Holy Spirit. This is the shape of our prayer; this is the pattern of our movement within the divine life of the Trinity. To this prayer all the people say, *"Amen."* Our hearts and minds and bodies and souls should be behind the word that sounds from our tongue. We say Amen as we proclaim as one to the Father, through the Son, in the Holy Spirit.

From the Liturgy of the Word we grow in wisdom
and from the Liturgy of the Eucharist in holiness.

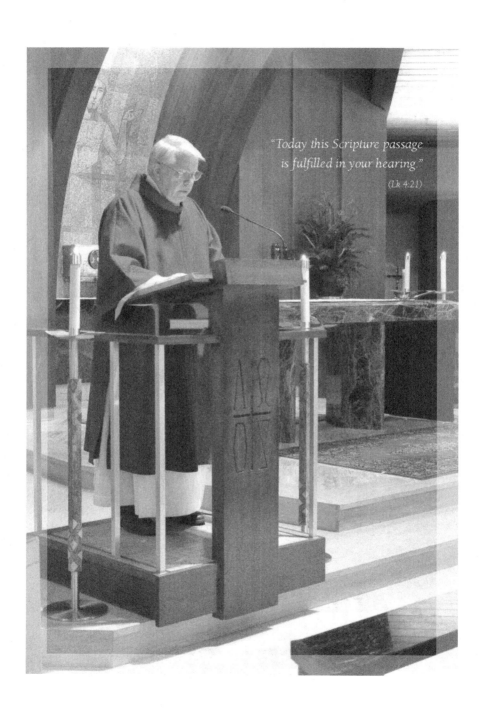

Lesson 2

Liturgy of the Word: Tell the Stories

"Today this Scripture passage is fulfilled in your hearing." (Luke 4:21)

Think of this verse as a gift from our host Jesus to you. As you hear the Word of God in this liturgy, Scripture is fulfilled not merely as a past historical event but today, here and now. There grows an essential bond between the Word of God and you in the celebration of Mass. Ancient hopes and expectations are fulfilled *"today in your hearing."* Hearing is a movement: the Word received moves from the physical ear to the mental, then to the spiritual. Every time the assembly hears the Word of God the community is spiritually enriched by the Word with new meaning and power.

Even the casual observer of the Liturgy of the Word will notice its shape and structure. We begin with a reading from the Old Testament, except during the Easter season when the first reading is from the Acts of the Apostles. The Easter season is but one season about which the liturgical year calendar revolves. The purpose of the liturgical year calendar is not to mark the passage of time, but to celebrate and understand more fully the entire mystery of Jesus metered out in what we refer to as vertical salvation history.

We then continue with a psalm; then a reading from the Epistles, followed by the Gospel acclamation, the Gospel proclamation and finally the homily. The Epistles are the twenty-one books of the New Testament following the four Gospels written in the form of letters to churches or individuals.

The "General Introduction to the Lectionary" (GIL) teaches us the significance of the Word of God in the liturgy: The many riches contained in the one Word of God are admirably brought out in the different kinds of liturgical celebration and in the different gatherings of the faithful who take part in those celebrations. This takes place as the unfolding mystery of Christ is recalled during the course of the liturgical year, as the Church's *sacraments* and *sacramentals* are celebrated, or as the faithful respond individually to the Holy Spirit working within them. The liturgical celebration, founded primarily on the Word of God and sustained by it, becomes a new event and enriches the "word" itself with new meaning and power. Thus in the liturgy the Church faithfully adheres to the way Christ himself read and explained the sacred Scriptures, beginning with the "today" of His coming forward in the synagogue and urging all to search the Scriptures. (Luke 4:16-21)[15]

However, what the casual observer may not notice is that every time the Word of God is heard, the heart is stirred in a different way. That is because God's Word, alive and active, is given through the power of the Holy Spirit. The Word of God is living and effective and expresses the Father's love that never fails. In the celebration of the Liturgy the Word of God is not announced in only one way nor does it always stir the hearts of the hearers with the same efficacy. Always, however, Christ is present in His "word" as He carries out the mystery of salvation, sanctifies humanity and offers the Father perfect worship. Moreover, the Word of God unceasingly calls to mind and extends the economy of salvation, which achieves its fullest expression in the liturgy. The liturgical celebration therefore becomes the continuing, complete, and effective presentation of God's Word. The Word of God constantly proclaimed in the liturgy always is a living and effective "Word" through the power of the Holy Spirit. It expresses the Father's love that never fails in its effectiveness toward us.[16]

> *"Sharper than any double-edged sword, it penetrates even to dividing soul and spirit, joints and marrow; it judges the thoughts and attitudes of the heart." (Heb 4:12)*

In proclaiming both the Old and New Testament, we remember that the whole of salvation history, all the way back to the beginning of Genesis, is but one mystery of salvation through Jesus Christ our Messiah. The New Testament lies hidden in the Old and the Old is illuminated in the New. Indeed, Christ is coeternal with the Father and is at the center and is the fullness of the whole of Scripture, Old and New, just as He is here and now the center and fullness of the Mass.

Just as Jesus promised the Samaritan woman at the well, He becomes the living waters we drink so that we might thirst no more.

---

[15] GIL – "General Introduction to the Lectionary" (Second Edition)
[16] GIL Paragraph 4.

"Everyone who drinks this water will be thirsty again, but whoever drinks the water I give them will never thirst. Indeed, the water I give them will become in them a spring of water welling up to eternal life." (John 4:13-14)

Thus, over time we are imbued with a profound wisdom and understanding of the celebration of the liturgy. With this increase in wisdom comes a reliance on God's Word. The Word of God recalls the mystery of Christ and our salvation. In its hearing, this mystery is carried forward in time where Christ is with us always, *"even to the very end of the age." (Matthew 28)* Christ himself is the center and fullness of the whole of Scripture, just as He is of all liturgical celebration. Thus the Scriptures are the living waters from which all who seek life and salvation must drink. The more profound our understanding of the celebration of the liturgy the higher is our appreciation of the importance of God's Word. Whatever we say of the one we can say of the other because each recalls the mystery of Christ and each in its own way causes the mystery to be carried forward. [17]

As your heart is stirred at hearing the Word of God, so is the heart of the assembly. In this way, the Church is built up and grows. God's Word speeds on and His name is glorified. We become a new people who trust in an ancient covenant, sanctified in Scripture and today perfected and fulfilled in our hearing. Through God's Word we long to have our hearts set on fire and yearn for the heavenly feast where our true joy lies. Through our active participation in hearing the Word of God we receive the grace to become His messengers to the world through the witness of our lives. GIL Paragraph 7 reads: "In the hearing of God's Word the Church is built up and grows and in the signs of the liturgical celebration God's wonderful past works in the history of salvation is presented anew as mysterious realities." God in turn makes use of the congregation of the faithful that celebrates the liturgy in order that His "Word" may speed on and be glorified and that His name be exalted among the nations. Whenever the Church gathered by the Holy Spirit for liturgical celebration announces and proclaims the Word of God she is aware of being a new people in whom the covenant made in the past is perfected and fulfilled. Baptism and confirmation in the Spirit have made all Christ's faithful into messengers of God's Word because of the grace of hearing they have received. Therefore

---

[17] GIL Paragraph 5.

they must be the bearers of the same "Word" in the Church and in the world by the witness of their lives. The Word of God proclaimed in the celebration of God's mysteries does not only address present conditions but looks back to past events and forward to what is yet to come. Thus God's Word shows us what we should hope for with such a longing that in this changing world our hearts will be set on the place where our true joy dwells.

The working of the Holy Spirit is ever present. It is that which *"penetrates even to dividing soul and spirit."* It gives inspiration and support and lifts the Word of God to preeminence as the foundation of the Mass and guidepost for our life. Remember that we are, in the words of Saint Paul in his First Letter to the Corinthians, Chapter 12, the Body of Christ through the Holy Spirit speaks to each of us individually and helps us find our place within Christ's body by fostering and bonding our diversity of gifts to share with our family, community and the world.

The working of the Holy Spirit is needed if the word of God is to make what we hear outwardly have its effect inwardly. Because of the Holy Spirit's inspiration and support, the word of God becomes the foundation of the liturgical celebration and the rule and support of all our life. The working of the Holy Spirit precedes, accompanies, and brings to completion the whole celebration of the Liturgy. But the Spirit also brings home to each person individually everything that in the proclamation of the word of God is spoken for the good of the whole gathering of the faithful. In strengthening the unity of all, the Holy Spirit at the same time fosters a diversity of gifts and furthers their multiform operation.[18]

You might ask if the Liturgy of the Word is sufficient to feed the world. It is of course not, yet it is a necessity. The preaching of the "Word" is necessary for the ministry of the sacraments of faith from which they are born and nourished. Its place in the Mass, then, is to prepare the way that leads us to the Eucharist. Scripture re-presents for us the sacrifice of the New Covenant and the banquet of grace that is the Eucharist. That is why the two-fold action of the "Word" proclaimed and the Eucharist received is but one single act of divine worship and praise to God that makes available this day the fullness of redemption.

---

[18] GIL 9.

The Church has honored the Word of God and the Eucharistic mystery with the same reverence, although not with the same worship, and always has and everywhere insisted upon and sanctioned such honor. Moved by the example of its founder, the Church has never ceased to celebrate His Paschal Mystery by coming together to read "what referred to Him in all the Scriptures" (Luke 24:27) and to carry out the work of salvation through the celebration of the memorial of the Lord and through the sacraments. "The preaching of the word is necessary for the ministry of the sacraments, for these are sacraments of faith, born and nourished from the word."[19]

The Church is nourished spiritually at the twofold table of God's word and of the Eucharist: from the one it grows in wisdom and from the other in holiness.

In the Word of God the divine covenant is announced; in the Eucharist the new and everlasting covenant is renewed. On the one hand, the history of salvation is brought to mind by means of human sounds; on the other, it is made manifest in the sacramental signs of the liturgy. The divine word read and proclaimed by the Church in the liturgy has as its one purpose the sacrifice of the New Covenant and the banquet of grace, that is, the Eucharist. The celebration of Mass, in which the "Word" is heard and the Eucharist is offered and received, forms but one single act of divine worship. That act offers the sacrifice of praise to God and makes available to God's creatures the fullness of redemption.

First Reading
The reader goes to the ambo and reads the First Reading, while all sit and listen.

While the Gospel is the center of the Liturgy of the Word it has its roots in the Old Testament. The Old Testament is a vast collection of theological traditions developed during well over a thousand years. Yet, despite the differences of the many human circumstances and authors that are reflected there, it is not difficult for the one who reads with faith to see that the collection as a whole leads to a the Gospel as its center. The central event for the Jews of the Old Testament was the Exodus, the wandering in the desert and the coming into the Promised Land. All things either led to that, recounted that, or looked back to that. The whole of revelation for

---

[19] GIL 10

Israel is focused in what God manifested himself to be in these events. Every subsequent generation remembered and celebrated them, defined their relationship with God in reference to them. Jesus, as a Jewish man, would have done the same. These events, then, become directly part of who He is. He expresses himself in terms of them. This is especially true of the days leading up to His Death and culminating in it.

When a passage from the Old Testament is read (i.e.: *remembered*[20]) at Mass, for Christians it is always from the perspective of the Christian central event of the passion of Jesus Christ. The Christian community hears it and associates it with the presence of the risen Lord. What happens at Mass in this moment was expressed already in the Gospel of Luke where the story of the risen Lord's appearance to the two disciples along the road to Emmaus is recounted. *"Jesus said, 'Everything written about me in the Law of Moses and the prophets and psalms had to be fulfilled.' Then He opened their minds to the understanding of the scriptures. He said to them: 'Thus it is written that the Messiah must suffer and rise from the dead on the third day'"* (Luke 24:44-46). The Lord, as prophet and Messiah teaches that He is the prophet written about in Israel's Scriptures as prophet and Messiah to be sent to the nation. Jesus is that central figure of Messiah, who must suffer so to enter into glory through the Cross and Resurrection.

The actual proclamation of the Word during Mass has its own power by virtue of its being announced and actively listened to. Those who actively listen will receive the Word as it penetrates their mind and heart. Then, through the sensorial faculty of active listening, it mysteriously begins to shape the person through reflection into this pattern of suffering and glory, illuminating the connection between the patterns of our lives and the biblical patterns.

---

[20] This power of remembering is called ANAMNESIS: The "remembrance" of God's saving deeds in history in the liturgical action of the Church, which inspires thanksgiving and praise.

These movements of Active Listening and Reflection are the first movements of *Lectio Divina*.[21] In this way we become a community which discovers that the meaning of our personal existence, and indeed, the meaning of the whole world, which cannot be understood apart from the great patterns of the sacred text. The Word is ever new. We don't leave our lives and our moment in history behind as we listen to these stories from the past; we actually take them up anew in the light of the Word we have heard. The story of our lives is seen to be part of a larger story, the story that the Bible tells.

In order for the congregation to be properly disposed to actively listen, the Reader at the ambo must take seriously the Ministry of Lector with a profound discipline, for this ministry is one of the great privileges of our Baptism. The listener receiving the Word should marvel at the grace that enables one of us to stand up and be used as an instrument through which the holy and life-giving Word of God is announced in the assembly. The Reader must take on this responsibility prayerfully so that the Word will effectively be proclaimed. As a ministry, the Reader must be imbued with a holiness of life and not merely an expertise in rhetorical technique.

At the end of the proclamation of the passage, the Reader declares what it is that we have just heard: *"The word of the Lord."* The declaration should be heard with absolute amazement as the congregation cries out from the depths of their hearts, *"Thanks be to God."* A few moments of silence follows, a time for wonder, awe and adoration in the presence of God who has spoken to us. A time to grasp that in this reading God's promises are fulfilled in Christ.

Responsorial Psalm
The psalmist or cantor sings or says the Psalm, with the people making the response.

Following this moment of reflection, our response is the words of the psalms. The psalms have been prayed and chanted throughout all periods

---

[21] *Lectio Divina*, translated as *Sacred Scripture*, has five movements, of which *Lectio* - Active Listening (or reading) and *Meditatio* – Reflecting on the reading, are the first two movements. *Oratio* – Prayer of a Grateful Heart, *Centemplatio* –resting within the Sacred Heart of Jesus, and *Operatio* – being sent in mission complete the five movements.

of history, for the people of Israel back a millennium or more before Christ, and forward through each century of our own Christian Story.

In the psalms are embodied the prayers of a people who heard God speaking in the creation and in the events of her history. They express joy and wonder, gratitude and repentance, pleas for help and mercy and protection. The psalms pray a Spirit-inspired response to the patterns of history as these patterns take on ever clearer shape and form. With the coming of Jesus Christ, the psalms shift onto a new level of meaning which refers entirely to Him and His story as the center of Israel's story.

Recalling the direction of the twofold movement of the liturgy spoken of earlier, in the First Reading God speaks to us, and in the Responsorial Psalm we respond to God with Christ in the middle as mediator. In this setting it is most effective when the psalm is chanted by a cantor.

Second Reading
If there is to be a Second Reading, a reader reads it from the ambo, as above.

As the New Testament authors emerged with their Letters starting in the mid first century, they matured within a Jewish life and heritage as represented in the Old Testament text. They used their Old Testament experience as a sort of springboard and platform into this new Christian era. Jesus becomes the new center for the New Testament writings. As we look at the content of the preaching of the earliest written work, that of Saint Paul, the Death and Resurrection of Jesus and the impact of on the early life of the disciples was the predominant message, without reference to the many words, parables, miracles of Jesus, not to mention the details of His birth. Christ's words were passed down from generation to generation in a rich oral tradition. With the passage of time, into the early second century, communities felt the need to commit the Oral Tradition to writing so as to permanently record a more extended narrative of the life of Jesus.

> *"Many have undertaken to draw up an account of the things that have been fulfilled among us, just as they were handed down to us by those who from the first were eyewitnesses and servants of the word. With this in mind, since I myself have carefully investigated everything from the beginning, I too decided to write an orderly account for you… so that you may know the certainty of the things you have been taught." Luke 1:1-4*

From this Oral Tradition the four Gospels arise. In the case of

Matthew and Luke this need reaches back to the very origins and birth of Jesus. But in every case, whatever was narrated about Jesus from the marvelous details surrounding His birth, or the words and deeds of His active ministry, had as its purpose placing the mystery of His Passion in a fuller context. It is within this context that we see the distinctive quality of the Second Reading and its role in the liturgy.

From the psalm we shift back to where God speaks again to His Church, and the Church listens. But now God's language is no longer the creation and the history of Israel. He speaks to us through the reflective writings of the Lord's chosen apostles. Through the Apostles, this contemplative moment provide us with penetrating reflections on the central message of the Gospel. We now experience, as did the early Christians, the reflective effort to absorb all that had been experienced in the Death and Resurrection of Jesus. The early theology of the Church emerged over a period of decades, illuminating for these believers an unimaginably profound sharing in the Lord's Passion and victory. The early Christian writers, with their deep knowledge of the Old Testament, masterfully enmeshed the old with new. A canon of New Testament texts emerged from this new Christian genre, documenting the living faith that was passed on to us from the apostles as the eyewitnesses of the Death and Resurrection of Jesus. That which became our canonical texts are considered inspired through the Holy Spirit, leading us to this understanding as God intended. Therefore, at this second reading of the Mass when the writings of an apostle are proclaimed the assembly is led to that moment where they can grasp the mystery. This interior understanding is what God is now saying to His people.

In the silence that follows this reading, in this new content delivered and grasped, Jesus Christ himself is moving deep into the hearts and minds of His people. He is pleased to do so through the words of His apostles, for He has entrusted all that He is, His entire mission, to them. *"As the Father has sent me into the world, so I send you."* (John 20:21)

Jesus purposefully designed His whole message to be spoken through the apostles and their faithfulness to what they receive from him. After only a brief period in the 40 days leading up to His Ascension the risen Lord lets himself be seen, then He ascends to the heavens, after which everything depends on the apostles who witnessed His Resurrection. Recall the words Jesus spoke to Mary in John 20:17 *"Do not hold on to me, for I have not yet ascended to the Father. Go instead to my brothers and tell them, 'I am ascending to my Father and your Father, to my God and your God.'"* Those who believe, although they have never seen Christ, believe not because they have seen the risen Lord, but because they believe what the apostles witness to. On the day of Pentecost the power of the Holy Spirit rushed upon these potentially disappointing figures and made them instead powerful witnesses. Generation after generation for two thousand years we now receive this Good News from our encounter with them. We believe what the apostles believed. We encounter the risen Lord through them, and pass on as the witness in every generation to follow. In making everything depend on the apostles, our risen Lord teaches us His intention to be one body with His Church. He is teaching us that He lives and acts only through her. He appears in His one, holy, catholic, and apostolic Church for all to encounter.

To indicate the end of the reading, the reader acclaims: The Word of the Lord. Assembly replies: Thanks be to God.

Gospel Preparation Prayers

The Presider bows before the altar and says quietly:
> *"Cleanse my heart and my lips, almighty God, that I may worthily proclaim your Gospel."*

If a Deacon of the Word is assisting, He bows before the Presider while the Presider prays:
> *"May the Lord be in your heart and on your lips, that you may proclaim His Gospel worthily and well, in the name of the Father, and of the Son, + and of the Holy Spirit."*

The deacon signs himself and replies: *"Amen."*

Alleluia or Gospel Acclamation
There follows the "Alleluia" or another chant as the liturgical time requires.

Following the Second Reading, we prepare for the proclamation of the Gospel, the joyful source and summit of the Liturgy of the Word. After a brief moment of quietude, all rise and sing the *"Alleluia!"* acclamation, in celebration of the Lord's Resurrection.

If incense is used, its smoke and sweet smell permeate the sanctuary while a procession forms. After praying over the Deacon of the Word, the Presider directs him to pick up the Book of the Gospels from the altar and take it to the Ambo. All these are mysteries. Through them the transcendent Lord speaks directly to His Church.

Gospel Proclamation

The deacon or priest then proceeds to the ambo. With his thumb, he signs the Gospel, and his forehead, praying sub vocal,
"May the Lord be in my mind, on my lips, and in my heart."

Then to the congregation he says:
"The Lord be with you."

Assembly replies: *"And with your spirit."*

Presider says: *"A reading from the holy Gospel according to …"*

Assembly replies: *"Glory to you, O Lord."*

At the end of the Gospel the deacon or priest acclaims:
"The Gospel of the Lord."

Assembly replies: *"Praise to you, Lord Jesus Christ."*

When Jesus rises from the dead, everything He ever said rises with him. By means of the reading of some particular passage from the Gospel text, the Church in her wisdom calls forth for the community a selected Gospel proclaiming a message of hope that has risen with Jesus. "Risen" is not some abstract concept, or some vague presence. The one who actually said and did these things, the one who was crucified and buried is the one who is risen and is present here and now in the proclamation. The Gospel is always about the Death and Resurrection of Jesus. Whatever else it tells has as its purpose placing the mystery of His Passion in its fuller context.

Because the Gospels are apostolic texts the faith that comes to us through the apostles applies also to our listening to and accepting what we hear in the Gospel reading. The difference is in the actual genre of the writings. The Second Reading is taken from one of the apostolic letters. The gospel genre, as mentioned earlier in this lesson, arose several decades later in order to meet a growing need in the life of the first communities, the need for a more extended narrative of the life of Jesus. This would keep the focus on the Death and Resurrection found in the letters from turning into an abstraction. There was much to remember about Jesus' whole life, and numerous Oral Traditions from it were naturally in circulation. There were His many memorable words and encounters with others, His marvelous parables, the miracles He worked from kindness and compassion, His various practices, most notably His habit of "*eating and drinking with sinners*" (see Luke 15:2).

The Church through the Holy Spirit recognized as the living faith the four Gospels that were eventually woven into the canon along with the Letters circulated by the apostles. These authors from the apostolic era gathered particular stories into a certain order and told a whole story emphasizing particular theological points useful to the communities for which they wrote. What we find in common with all those who traced the whole sequence of events from the beginning is that they all agree that the center and climax of the story is the Death and Resurrection of Jesus. Whatever is told is part of this story and helps us to deepen our grasp of it.

As we hear the Gospel being proclaimed, we should be aware that this is not just that particular deacon or priest standing at the ambo and reading out loud. The proclamation of the Gospel is a mystery, and through it something is happening in this moment. Jesus himself visits the assembly in human form, speaking to us in the words proclaimed, performing miracles, telling parables, eating and drinking with sinners. Whatever particular Gospel we hear on a given day leads us that day toward the Central Historical Event. What is ultimately happening is that Jesus is present to the assembly as the one who was crucified and is now risen. In the Gospel of John, Jesus refers to His Death and Resurrection as His "hour." His hour is an hour that never passes away, never fades into the past or old with the passage of time. His hour is what is happening when the Gospel is read. He is present with His sacrifice, as the one whose entire life in all its details led inexorably to this Death of which all the Law and Prophets spoke. He is the one present now, for He has risen from the dead. When we begin the Liturgy of the Eucharist, we will see that the ritual and words of that part of the Mass say and accomplish in their own way what has already been said in the Liturgy of the Word. They intensify the character of the one event that is the center of all: the Death and Resurrection of Jesus.

Imbedded in the proclamation and in this holy remembrance is the mystical power of the Gospel event to be lifted from the past to our present. What Jesus once said and did becomes present in our midst as the Gospel is read: this event of Christ becomes the event of this particular community here and now. Christ comes and is received as an instrument of salvation to the particular assembly that here and now hears this Word. It is a saving word for us, full of power, and new because this particular community hearing this Gospel event in these circumstances has never existed before.

In the proclamation of the Gospel there is an intensification and climax of the movement of God the Father toward the world. Expressed in terms of its Trinitarian and ecclesial shape, what the Father says to the Church is Jesus Christ. When we hear Him, when we see Him act, we should be mindful that this is the Father's Word given to us. What He says and does reveals the Father as does His Death and Resurrection. This Word reaches its mark in the hearts of those who hear it because it comes accompanied by the Holy Spirit, just as Christ first came into the world accompanied by the Spirit. The Spirit ensures that Jesus Christ is infused into the community which stands in reverence, wonder and awe. At its conclusion we cry out to the one who is now present among us: *"Praise to you, Lord Jesus Christ!"*

The Homily

The homily is ordinarily given by the Presider. He may also entrust it to a concelebrating priest or to the Deacon of the Word.

The Church has honored the Word of God and the Eucharistic mystery with the same reverence, although not with the same worship, and always has and everywhere insisted upon and sanctioned such honor. Moved by the example of its founder, the Church has never ceased to celebrate His Paschal Mystery by coming together to read *"what referred to Him in all the Scriptures"* (Luke 24:27) and to carry out the work of salvation through the celebration of the memorial of the Lord and through the sacraments.

"The preaching of the word is necessary for the ministry of the sacraments, for these are sacraments of faith, which is born and nourished from the word." [22]

In the Word of God the divine covenant is announced; in the Eucharist the new and everlasting covenant is renewed. On the one hand, the history of salvation is brought to mind by means of human sounds; on the other, it is made manifest in the sacramental signs of the liturgy. It can never be forgotten, therefore, that the divine word read and proclaimed by

---

[22] See GIL paragraph 10

the Church in the liturgy has as its one purpose the sacrifice of the New Covenant and the banquet of grace, that is, the Eucharist. The celebration of Mass, in which the "Word" is heard and the Eucharist is offered and received, *forms but one single act of divine worship.* That act offers the sacrifice of praise to God and makes available to God's creatures the fullness of redemption.

The unique nature of the homily is captured well in St. Luke's account of Christ's preaching in the synagogue of Nazareth (cf. Luke 4:16-30). After reading a passage from the Prophet Isaiah He handed the scroll back to the attendant and began, *"Today this Scripture has been fulfilled in your hearing."* The homilist breaks open the Word for the people, such that Christ's Paschal Mystery is proclaimed: preparing the community to celebrate the Eucharist, and to recognize that in this celebration they truly share in the mystery of the Lord's death and Resurrection. Then the members of the community, transformed by the Eucharist, can carry the Gospel into the world in their daily lives.

Rev. David Rosenberg

I HAVE TOLD YOU THIS SO THAT MY JOY MIGHT BE IN YOU AND YOUR JOY MIGHT BE COMPLETE.[i]

Lesson 3

The Creed and Universal Prayer of the People

The Creed: Our Profession of Faith

God's Commitment to Us and Our Response of Faith

God speaks to us in the Scriptures. He tells us who He is. In the Gospels, we come to know Jesus the Lord. We learn of His charity and hear His call to righteousness. His relationship to the Father and the Spirit is revealed in what He tells us. It is a relationship of love. God, the Father, Son and Holy Spirit invite us through the Word to share their loving relationship. The Spirit is poured out into our hearts to enable us to stand in right relationship with God and entrust out entire being to Him through the creed.

Our assembled community stands together and responds by pledging its commitment to God and belief in His identity. Each individual begins their response by saying, *"I believe,"* *'Credo'* in Latin. We say firmly that the physical universe is created not an accident. We say that the creator is Father to His creation; His beloved Son was begotten not made; His divine Son sent into the world for our salvation joined us in our humanity. We say we know that the Father and the Son have sent the Spirit to abide in us. We announce our confidence in God. What we have heard Him say in the proclaimed Scriptures we believe. We recognize our Lord and He recognizes us in our assent. We recognize each other as members of a single community when we say together we believe the same things concerning God. We share a common heritage; father, mother, brothers and sisters, a spirit and a future. We are children of one Father and siblings of His Son. We are a family, the family of God.

The Creed, like the last book of the Bible, ends with the Hebrew word *"Amen."* This word frequently concludes prayers in the New Testament. The Church, likewise, ends her prayers with *"Amen."* In Hebrew, *"Amen"* comes from the same root as the word *"believe."* This root expresses solidarity, trustworthiness, faithfulness. And so, we can understand why *"Amen"* may express both God's faithfulness towards us and our trust in him.

In the book of the Prophet Isaiah, we find the expression "God of truth" (literally "God of the Amen"), that is, the God who is faithful to His promises: *"He who blesses himself in the land shall bless himself by the God of truth. Amen."* Our Lord often used the word "Amen," sometimes repeated to emphasize the trustworthiness of His teaching, His authority founded on God's truth.

The creed's final "Amen" repeats and confirms its first words: "I believe." To believe is to say "Amen" to God's words, promises and commandments; to entrust oneself completely to Him who is the "Amen" of infinite love and perfect faithfulness. The Christian's life will then be the "Amen" to the "I believe" of our baptismal profession of faith: May your creed be for you as a mirror. Look at yourself in it, to see if you believe everything you say you believe. And rejoice in your faith each day.[23]

The baptismal origins of the Creed are important reminders to us that Baptism and the faith into which we were plunged at Baptism are the only doors through which we can enter into the Liturgy of the Eucharist which is about to begin. The Creed is the Church's ultimate response of faith to God's movement toward her. In each particular Eucharistic assembly that recites it, every baptized person confirms again his or her belonging to the community that believes these things. This is the community, larger and older than the sum of the parts gathered, that is about to celebrate the Eucharist. How tremendous is the Amen that resounds at the end of the Creed, echoing round the globe, echoing through the centuries, echoing in the halls of heaven.

Beginning in the first century a pledge of belief in articles of faith arranged as lists of beliefs has been used during baptismal rites. Over the centuries, the simple first century baptismal lists were expanded by the addition of material, which clarified the original content but never changed it. There are two primary forms of this pledge of assent. One is a first century formulation, the Apostles' Creed. The other is a fourth century document, the Nicene Creed. Every Christian denomination begins its constitutional formulas with adherence to these creedal statements. They are the signs that identify the authenticity of someone who claims to be a Christian.

Legend has it that the Apostles' Creed, the "Creed of Creeds," was written by the Apostles on the day of Pentecost, the tenth day after Christ's ascension into heaven. While still under the direct inspiration of the Holy Spirit, each of the Apostles contributed one of the 12 articles. Even though

---

[23] See CCC 1061-1064

this is an undocumented legend, the name stuck. Each of the doctrines found in the creed can be traced to statements current in the apostolic period. The earliest written version of the creed is perhaps the "Interrogatory Creed of Hippolytus." (ca. AD 215) Hippolytus' version is given in question and answer format with the baptismal candidates answering in the affirmative that they believed each statement.

It is the one Spirit received at baptism that makes a diverse collection of human beings the Church. The pledge of faith always has contained an affirmation of the effects of the presence of the Holy Spirit in the baptized individual, which are forgiveness of sins, resurrection of the dead and the eternal life for those raised from the dead.

At each Sunday Mass, we pledge through the recitation of the creed that we are faithful to this ancient proclamation. Our pledge enables us to enter that portion of the Eucharistic celebration that feeds and sustains our faith. Through the creed, we move from the Liturgy of the Word to the Liturgy of the Eucharist.

NICENE CREED	APOSTLES' CREED
I believe in one God, the Father almighty, maker of heaven and earth, of all things visible and invisible. I believe in one Lord Jesus Christ, the Only Begotten Son of God, born of the Father before all ages. God from God, Light from Light, true God from true God, begotten, not made, consubstantial with the Father; through Him all things were made. For us men and for our salvation He came down from heaven, and by the Holy Spirit was incarnate of the Virgin Mary, and became man. For our sake He was crucified under Pontius Pilate, He suffered death and was buried, and rose again on the third day in accordance with the Scriptures. He ascended into heaven and is seated at the right hand of the Father. He will come again in glory to judge the living and the dead and His kingdom will have no end. I believe in the Holy Spirit, the Lord, the giver of life, who proceeds from the Father and the Son, who with the Father and the Son is adored and glorified, who has spoken through the prophets. I believe in one, holy, catholic and apostolic Church. I confess one Baptism for the forgiveness of sins and I look forward to the resurrection of the dead and the life of the world to come. Amen.	I believe in God, the Father Almighty, Creator of Heaven and earth, and in Jesus Christ, His only Son, our Lord, who was conceived by the Holy Spirit, born of the Virgin Mary, suffered under Pontius Pilate, was crucified, died, and was buried. He descended into hell; on the third day He arose again from the dead; He ascended into heaven and is seated at the right hand of God the Father Almighty, from hence He shall come to judge the living and the dead. I believe in the Holy Spirit, the holy catholic Church, the communion of saints, the forgiveness of sins, the resurrection of the body, and life everlasting. Amen.

Universal Prayer of the Faithful

Trust in God and Heart for the Needs of the World

"We look forward to a new heaven and a new earth, where righteousness dwells. So then, dear friends, since you are looking forward to this, make every effort to be found spotless, blameless and at peace with him." (2 Pt 3:13-14)

God, Lord of life and love, is our Father. We have heard it proclaimed and we have announced our belief. As children of a loving Father, we demonstrate our belief in Him by asking our Father for good things. We long to be righteous and holy, a holiness that draws us in humility to ask this not for ourselves but for the Church and for the world. In petitioning him, we demonstrate our confidence in His mercy and His love revealed in the sacrifice of His Son, which we have gathered to remember.

In the Roman Missal that contains the texts and ritual instructions for Mass the clear order of the Eucharistic liturgy is laid out, with a precisely located shift from the Liturgy of the Word to the Liturgy of the Eucharist. The last part of the Liturgy of the Word is the *Universal Prayer, the Prayer of the Faithful*.

The Presider opens with an introduction and invitation for the people to pray. The Presider, a sacrament of Christ as the head of His body, leads the people in prayer. The movement is a movement of the assembly toward God the Father. Christ stands as mediator. Our coming to the Father is through him. Then the Deacon of the Word, if assisting the Presider, or an appointed lay person articulates particular prayers on behalf of the assembly, and the assembly adds its own voice to each one together. This series of petitions creates a pulsing rhythm as the Church cries out her needs before the heavenly Father.

These are called the Universal Prayer, as an indication of the direction in which our prayer ought to go. Individuals can pray for their particular needs in the quiet of their hearts. Here the Church is giving voice to her relationship with the whole world. These intercessions are also called the Prayer of the Faithful because it is the responsibility of the baptized persons who live in the world to bring before God in prayer the needs of the Church and the whole world. It is precisely their life in the world, enlightened and shaped by what they have heard today in the Word of God, which equips these people with knowledge of what to pray for.

In the Prayer of the Faithful, the pattern for use at Mass reminds us that the local Church gathered in prayer is united with the universal Church.

The recommended order for intentions given in the "Roman Missal" is as follows:
- For the needs of the Church
- For the world
- For those in need
- For the local community
- For the deceased

We respond after each intention. Reader: "Let us pray to the Lord." Assembly replies: "Lord hear our prayer."

As we again consider at this juncture the twofold movement of the liturgy, we note that God addresses the world not vaguely but through the Church. The Church exists for the sake of the world and speaks a word of response to God in the name of the whole world. At this moment in the liturgy the direction is a movement of response to God's word on the part of the Church and for the sake of the world. It is this role of the Church that is articulated now in this prayer. The Presider invites the faithful to articulate the prayer as a ritual expression of mystery, of Christ entrusting to His Body a responsibility in the world. By His own example Christ has taught us what and whom to care about. Now He transforms us to have a heart and mind like His. This is nothing less than the sharing with us His priestly role of interceding for the world. After we have expressed our needs, Jesus will gather them together and make them His own as the Presider concludes the prayer: *"through Christ our Lord."*

At the conclusion of the Universal Prayer we close the Liturgy of the Word. Inquirers of the faith and *Catechumens*, those individuals preparing to be received into the Church at the Easter Vigil Mass, are formally dismissed at this point and the Liturgy of the Eucharist begins. Gifts of bread and wine, as well as other gifts, will be collected from the faithful and brought forward in procession to the Presider. Considering the Universal Prayer as a hinge, we can say that all that we have prayed for will be brought forward with the bread and wine and placed as sacrifice in Christ's hands for transformation. The Church brings both herself and the world forward and petitions transformation.

Rev. David Rosenberg

"Andrew, the brother of Simon Peter, said to Jesus, 'There is a boy here who has five barley loaves and two fish; but what good are these for so many?'" (Jn 6:3)

LESSON 4

THE BARAKAH –
OFFERING THE FRUIT OF THE EARTH AND WORK OF HUMAN HANDS

Now that the assembly is fully united as one, with minds and hearts illuminated by the Word of God, we turn to the preparation of the altar and the offerings. Here offerings are freely presented as gifts to share with those in need. From the very beginning, Christians have brought gifts to share along with bread and wine for the Eucharist.

This custom of the collection, ever appropriate, is inspired by the example of Christ who became poor to make us rich. The money and any other currency that is collected is presented to the Presider to assist in the spirit of *"subsidiarity,"*[24] for orphans and widows, those whom illness or any other cause has deprived of resources, prisoners, immigrants and, in a word, all who are in need. *(See CCC 1351)*

In procession, the bread and wine are brought to the altar; they will be offered by the priest in the name of Christ in the Eucharistic sacrifice in which they will become His body and blood. It is the very action of Christ at the Last Supper – *"taking the bread and a cup."* Here the Church offers in thanksgiving that which comes forward from His creation.

The presentation of the offerings at the altar takes up the gesture of Melchizedek and commits the Creator's gifts into the hands of Christ who, in His sacrifice, brings to perfection all human attempts to offer sacrifices.[25]

My name will be great among the nations, from where the sun rises to where it sets. In every place incense and pure offerings will be brought to me. Mal 1:11

Scripture teaches us that there is a necessary spiritual reality to being childlike as we present our gifts to God. In Chapter 6 verse 5 of Johns Gospel, this was demonstrated by the boy who presented the meager gifts

---

[24] Subsidiarity: a principle of Catholic social doctrine that all social entities exist for the sake of the individual so that what individuals are able to do for one another, society should not take over, and what small community organizations can do, larger organizations should not take over.

[25] See CCC 1350

of five loaves and two fish to Jesus for feeding the five thousand. This presentation of the gifts is exactly what we do at every Mass, when we bring up a small amount of bread and wine insufficient to feed everyone. The priest receives these meager ritual offerings and acknowledges this fact as He blesses them using the ancient Jewish prayer of blessing called the *"Barakah."*

When Jesus received the gifts from the boy, as a Jewish ritual of His time, He would have raised the offering and, lifting His eyes heavenward, prayed a *"Barakah"* with similar words, *"Blessed are you Lord God of all creation. For through your goodness we have received the bread and fish we offer you: Fruit of the earth and work of human hands, it will become for us food for the journey."* And everyone present would have replied: *"Blessed be God forever."* This *barakah* is the ritual blessing passed down through the ages that the priest prays twice at every Mass, once over the bread and once over the wine.

The *"Barakah,"* is a reminder for us that everything we have is a gift from God, even the meager bread and wine we give back to Him. If we take a moment to turn our minds to a state of childlike wonder and awe at this ritual in the Mass, we can then appreciate the impact of the sacred blessings given and received.

> *"The Barakah is the intentional discipline of gratitude to acknowledge that all I am and have is given to me as a gift of love, a gift to be celebrated with joy."*

Church tradition holds to calling the Mass a *"sacrifice."* We need to understand the richness of this word concept that encapsulates all that *"the Sacrifice of the Mass"* means. This term *"sacrifice"* becomes clear as we break open how it is used throughout what follows.

> *"May we offer these good things that pass, so that we might hold fast to those that ever endure."*

> Bread is loaded with a rich symbolism that Jesus understood. Bread is the *"fruit of the earth"*. The bread points to the earth. It is clear from the Gospel that Jesus often pondered the grain of wheat. In the parable of the growing seed, He says: *"The earth produces of itself, first the blade, then the ear, then the full grain in the ear"* (Mk 4:28). When the grain falls into the earth, it draws energies from the earth itself. It lives and develops by the help of the earth's mysterious powers. The sprout needs all the powers of heaven: rain, light, warmth, wind. The development of the seed engages the entire physical world. By the fact that so many cosmic powers are involved in the grain of wheat's growth, it could be seen as a synthesis of the whole cosmos.

The bread is also the result of the sacrifice of "the work of human hands". There would not be bread if man did not sow, harvest, grind, knead, and bake. All of this work is or should be an expression of love. Man's work is, first of all, to nourish himself. But, unlike animals, man takes his nourishment in the form of a meal. And a meal means fellowship, love. Strictly speaking, man works, not to nourish himself, but, rather, to nourish his family and loved ones. We are created to give life to others, never to ourselves.

Actually, all of our work should be a work of sacrifice and love. We work with the physical world to make life easier, not primarily for ourselves, but for others. By our work, we create possibilities for deeper fellowship.

The Bread also has something to do with Jesus himself. He likens himself to a grain of wheat: "Unless a grain of wheat falls into the earth and dies, it remains alone; but if it dies, it bears much fruit" (John 12:24). The grain of wheat is entrusted to the earth but rises up later in the form of an ear. Where the original grain multiplies, so Jesus by dying and rising has brought a multitude of brothers and sisters who are like Him (Rom 8:29) and who, therefore, in their turn must follow the same law of death, resurrection, and fruitfulness.

To die in order to give life: that is what we can learn from the grain of wheat. We see in the Eucharist's form of bread that this sacrament has a sacrificial character. The bread symbolizes the whole cosmos, the work of all mankind, and Jesus himself.[26]

These fundamental symbols of the Eucharistic liturgy are not just natural symbols. They are in fact the product of the cooperation between the Creator *(fruit of the earth)* and human beings *(work of human hands.)*

It is true that bread and wine have their precise meaning in the context of the Passover and in the Lord's Last Supper and that bread and wine are involved here in obedience to His command to do this in memory of Him. But we can reflect as well on the fittingness of the Lord's choice and what the Spirit had prepared. Bread and wine in fact are extremely strong symbols, powerful and rich in what they express. Perhaps nothing summarizes so well the deepest experience of what it means to be a human being and what we most desire. Nonetheless, it is precisely in this condition of poverty before God that Christ comes to meet us and reveal His solidarity with us in this poverty. He will take our gifts into His hands, and He will transform them into His very Body and Blood, transform them into

---

[26] Quote from the book "Bread that is Broken pg 12; Wilfrid Stinnison; OCD; 2020 Ignatian Press ISBN 978-1-62164-317-3

His Paschal Sacrifice that He is continually offering in heaven. God's Word to us is Jesus Christ, and the action of His dying and rising. This Word will now be articulated to us in the syllables and words and phrases of bread and wine transformed. They become a language. The name of this language is flesh. It is our flesh, our lives, we who brought the gifts. Our gifts become the Word made flesh. Thereby the whole creation and the whole of history are rendered capable of something that, by definition, would be impossible to them. They are rendered capable of being God's expression of himself. They are rendered capable of being an offering to God the Father, of being the *"barakah"* and adoration that Christ's very sacrifice on the cross was and is. We offer up our lives to God, not by ourselves but only through Him and with Him and in Him in Christ's offering.

In the course of the rite when bread and wine are brought to the hands of Presider by the baptized, a magnificent exchange begins to take shape. We bring our lives with all our efforts to produce and to be together in love, with all our desire and our willingness to share, and we place them in the hands of Christ by placing them in the hands of the Presider who is in this moment the sacrament of Christ the head, who leads His whole body in offering His sacrifice.

WATER MIXED WITH WINE

The first of these mysteries is seen as the Deacon of the Cup or priest pours wine into the chalice and then mixes a little water into the wine as he does so. The words he says inaudibly call to mind the mystery of this action. He says,

> *"By the mystery of this water and wine may we come to share in the divinity of Christ, who humbled himself to share in our humanity."*

Early followers of Christ noticed in this a wonderful image for understanding our communion with the sacrifice of Christ. Of the two elements, wine and water, wine is to be the precious blood of Christ. Blood is the common bond among all humanity. The water placed in the wine represents the River of Life flowing from the pierced side of Christ that brings us the waters of baptism and initiates us as Adopted Children of the Father in mystical wonder and awe. As early as the middle of the third century Saint Cyprian of Carthage was talking this way. He said that we should never offer the wine without water since that would be like offering Christ without His people. It is a little gesture, but it has long been done and is a striking mystery.

INCENSE

The relation between the gifts presented and the faithful is manifested with special clarity in the liturgy when incense is used. First, the gifts are incensed, which is a ritual gesture marking them as holy. In this symbolic action our senses take in the mystery before us. Then the altar on which the gifts lie is designated as the holy place, the center of the world, the place of Christ's Paschal Sacrifice. Then the incensing shifts to bless the priest as head of the body, after which the assembly is incensed to indicate that they themselves are what lies on the altar in sacrifice.

CLEANSING THE SERVANT: THE HAND WASHING

"I wash my hands in innocence, and go about your altar, Lord, proclaiming aloud your praise and telling of all your wonderful deeds." (Ps 26:6-7)

After receiving and blessing the bread and wine, the Presider turns to the altar server holding the pitcher and bowl to wash his hands. This ritual washing is a visible acknowledgement of one's promise to live a chaste and holy life.

The earliest origin of this ritual is biblical, *"Then the Lord said to Moses, Make a bronze basin, with its bronze stand, for washing." (Ex 30:17-18)* This practice emerged as the Jewish ritual washing tradition called *"Netilat yadayim,"* which was done with the *"Barakah"* blessing prior to eating bread.

In the Liturgy of the Eucharist, the bowl and pitcher, called the *"lavabo"* (I shall wash) is derived from Psalm 26:6, *"I wash my hands in innocence. ...."* The priest inaudibly says, *"Lord, wash away my inequities and cleanse me from my sins."*

From the third and fourth centuries on it appears to have been usual for the ministers during the Mass to ceremonially wash their hands before the more solemn consecration as a symbol of inward purity.

Following the *Barakah* of bread and wine and ritual hand cleansing, the Presider calls the assembly to prayer:
"Pray, my brothers and sisters, that my sacrifice and yours may be acceptable to God, the almighty Father."

The assembly responds:
*"May the Lord accept the sacrifice at your hands
for the praise and glory of His name,*

*for our good
and the good of all His holy Church."*

SANCTIFYING THE ORDINARY: PRAYER OVER THE OFFERINGS

The special purpose of the *"Prayer over the Offerings"* is to ask God to receive the bread and wine to sanctify it and make it holy. *The "Prayer over the Offerings"* is chanted or recited by the celebrant and changes for each feast or occasion. It also asks for the intercessions of the saint of the day. This dates back to the earliest Prayer over the Offerings we know, around 450 A.D.

The presentation of the offerings at the altar takes up the gesture of Melchizedek and commits the Creator's gifts into the hands of Christ who, in His sacrifice, brings to perfection all human attempts to offer sacrifices. *(cf CCC 1350)*

The whole church becomes a sweet smelling prayer as the priest prays. When we say Amen to this prayer, we are saying Amen to all that has happened from the collecting of the gifts to this moment. Now we stand poised for the Eucharistic Prayer.

LESSON 5

The Preface: We are Called Together in His Name

Eucharistic Prayer: the Anaphora

The Anaphora: most solemn part of the Divine Liturgy, a thanksgiving prayer of acclaim and response for the offerings of bread and wine to be consecrated as the body and blood of Christ.

The *"Anaphora"* Eucharistic Prayer is the prayer of thanksgiving and consecration where we come to the source and summit of the celebration. In the Preface to the Eucharistic Prayer, the Church gives thanks to the Father, through Christ, in the Holy Spirit, for all his works: creation, redemption, and sanctification. The whole assembly joins in the unending praise that the Mystical Church sings to the thrice-holy God. *(cf CCC 1352)*

"Anaphora" is an ancient Common Greek (*"Koin"*) title dating back to the early Church when Greek was the common language. The Anaphora is a collection of *"anaphors."* The anaphor is a literary device (think of "metaphor" as another common literary device from the same *"koin"* era.) The anaphor is simply a framed acclaim and response collection used to actively engage the assembly in this sacred prayer. In the first anaphor of the invocation to the Preface, the Presider acclaims, *"The Lord be with you."* And the congregation responds, *"And with your spirit."* The "Anaphora," then, is the sacred collection of anaphors that ends with the assembly's great *"Amen"* prior to the Communion.

Immediately following the Presider's call to the assembly to prayer, he begins the Eucharistic prayer:

> Presider: "The Lord be with you."
> Assembly: "And with your spirit."
> Presider: "Lift up your hearts."
> Assembly: "We lift them up to the Lord."
> Presider: "Let us give thanks to the Lord our God."
> Assembly: "It is right and just."

The Presider then prays the Preface. From the Latin *"prae fatio"* the word preface literally means *"to pray in front of"* or *"proclaim in the presence of."* In the Preface, the Church gives thanks to the Father, through Christ, in the Holy

Spirit, for all His works.

With the Presider's words *"Lift up your hearts,"* we begin the holy task for which we have been called together. Our response, *"We have lifted them up,"* assures the priest, who stands in the place of our host, we are ready to begin. Then he announces the purpose of our assembly, *"Let us give thanks to the Lord our God."* Our response is a firm statement that *"It is right and just."*

Having received our assent to what God has called us to do, the priest repeats our words, *"It is right and just,"* and begins a prayer that enumerates the many ways that God has blessed us. The Preface is both an announcement of the purpose of our gathering and solidarity with Christ and His sacrifice. We give thanks to God for the many blessings bestowed on us because it is only right and just.

As mentioned a bit earlier, in the first anaphor the priest opens his arms wide and acclaims, *"The Lord be with you."* The assembly responds, *"And with your spirit."* This invocation is a call to pray with a much greater intensity and for this we humbly beg for divine inspiration as we offer the Church's greatest prayer.

Because of the central role of the priest in this prayer, the full and active attention of the assembly is required. His gestures as he offers the gifts and proclaims this powerful prayer can only be grasped by the assembly as they rise in wonder and awe. The assembly responds *"And with your spirit"* to stir the *"spirit"* of the priest, that deepest interior part of his being where he has been ordained precisely to lead the assembly in this sacred action. Now representing Christ, he must be attuned to attend to his sacred duties well. As his greeting is a blessing on the people, the people bless their priest in return. The people know that if their priest is *"in this prayer"* with all his heart, all his mind, all his soul, they, too, will be. In this prayer he is their leader, and they cannot rise in glory without him.

The priest's leading role throughout the entire Eucharistic Prayer is meant to make present through the senses for the assembly a fundamental reality that this is the most intense of prayers. That reality is that the Church addresses itself to the Father only through Christ its head. The priest is a sacrament of Christ signifying this reality. The whole structure of the prayer with the priest speaking and acting and the people following and saying their Amen at the end is an incarnate reality, yet a mystery, in which we experience Christ as head of the body leading His whole body before the Father. In this first of three *anaphor*s, priest and people have acknowledged and lovingly awakened each other to the roles they must play in what follows.

With the second *anaphor* "*Lift up your hearts,*" the priest, acting in *persona Christi Capitis* as Christ at the head of His body acclaims what is about to happen with authority, excitement and love. It is Christ the head telling His body that we are about to rise to the heavens, calling us to that full, active and conscious participation which is demanded by the very nature of the liturgy. *(cf SC14)*

The baptized faithful respond, *"We lift them up to the Lord."* We have been summoned upward, and our hearts are on fire to be lifted up. This summons on high is the inbreaking of the River of Life, meeting us at the altar, brought into this eternal moment of Christ's Resurrection, into His hour, where past and future are both made present to us, where we are meant to be for all eternity. Having our hearts on high releases us from our pragmatic anxieties and daily cares as we gain the perspective that allows us to see our ultimate meaning and purpose planted deep within us at the moment of our conception. We are obeying the apostle's injunction when he said, *"Since you have been raised up in company with Christ, set your heart on what pertains to higher realms where Christ is seated at God's right hand. Be intent on things above rather than on things of earth. After all, you have died! Your life is hidden now with Christ in God. When Christ our life appears, then you shall appear with Him in glory"* (Colossians 3:1-3).

The priest now acclaims our purpose, *"Let us give thanks to the Lord our God."* The assembly responds: *"It is right and just."* Within the dynamic of this third *anaphor*, we give thanks that our hearts are now on high in this hour of Christ's culmination of the mighty deeds worked for our salvation and gifted to us by the grace of God.

The priest leading this prayer images for the assembly the reality of Christ as head of His praying body. The phrase *"through Christ our Lord"* in the Preface, as well as the second part which expresses His action on our behalf.

The priest is a sacrament of Christ in his role as head. He is an image of Christ but is at the same time distinguishable from him. His is the voice of the assembly, the voice of the Church, speaking through Christ. Later we will see that during the narrative of the Lord's Supper, the priest will pronounce Christ's very words over the bread and wine, and in that moment he is "*in persona Christi* **Capitis**"[27] "*in the person of Christ* **the head**," a

---

[27] A priest is *in persona Christi* as he acts as Christ and as God. An extended

very sharp image of Christ. Christ now acts through him. What the priest does, as voice of the Church, he does through Christ.

These mighty deeds have a center, the Death and Resurrection of Christ, and we are now at the nexus of the greatest event in human history, the salvation of the world. So it is this for which we give thanks. Christ himself thanks His Father for his Resurrection, a thanksgiving which includes His joy that we can be made members of His risen body. We also thank the Father together with Him. The Eucharistic Prayer, our thanksgiving, follows. The Greek word, *Eucharist* literally means *Thanksgiving*.

THE PRIEST SPEAKS TO GOD

As soon as the assembly responds in unity, the priest focuses and directs all his attention to the One to whom the Eucharistic Prayer is addressed. From now until the end of the prayer, every word is addressed to God the Father and every gesture is performed in His presence.

Among the earth bound congregation a circular wind is stirring. As the focus is raised heavenward, the circular wind rises up to the heavens, and it returns, filling our sacred space with grace, a tsunami of grace that will permeate outward to the four corners of our community. The people follow their priest in his every word and gesture, aware, as the dialogue has expressed, that all of us together, priest and people, must keep our minds and hearts on high, tensed, strained, stretched, through to the end of this prayer, where the assembly, in the name of the whole creation, will sing their passionate Amen to all that has been accomplished.

> *The voice of the priest is the voice of the assembly, and the assembly has voice only in its priest, and there is only one priest: Jesus Christ.*

The assembly kneels with the elders in heaven. The priest stands before the throne of God joining in prayer the ongoing ever renewed thanksgiving of Christ offered up at the Last Supper and completed on Calvary.

---

term, *in persona Christi capitis*, "in the person of Christ the head," was introduced at the Vatican Council II in the Decree on the Ministry and Live of Priests, Presbyterorum Ordinis, December 7, 1965.

Rev. David Rosenberg

LESSON 6

Eucharistic Prayers and Consecration: Preparing the Sacrificial Meal

INVOCATION – INVITING THE POWER OF GOD

Standing before the throne of God the priest begins an intimate conversation with God asking Him to notice our actions and to send His power to transform the gifts we have gathered. The priest does not speak for himself alone but petitions God to bless what we offer noting that we do this in communion with those we venerate and as an offering for the Church, ourselves and those dear to us. *(cf Eucharistic Prayer I)* It is through the power of the Holy Spirit called down upon by the priest in the epiclesis that God has gathered us for himself from east to west, from the rising of the sun to its setting. *(Eucharistic Prayer III)* It is the power of that same Spirit that the Presider invokes to transform our gifts. *(cf Eucharistic Prayers II, III, IV)* In the Roman Rite there are two epicleses, both described in detail a little later in this chapter.

It is very important that the assembly be aware of its role as the priestly baptized to fully, consciously and actively participate in it. Active Listening and following the prayer is participation.

We participate in what Christ is accomplishing on our behalf. We go to the Father through Him. All our attention is required for this participation. We must keep our hearts fully engaged. We are already mindful of and reaching toward the great Amen, which we will all sing together to close this great prayer.

In the Roman rite since the time of the reform of the liturgy mandated by the Second Vatican Council, one of several different Eucharistic Prayers is chosen for any given celebration of Mass. Each of these prayers has a unique way of unfolding the Eucharistic mystery. All the prayers begin with a Preface. The priest then continues with words that acknowledge the glory of God. In acknowledging God we recall before Him the wonders of creation and the great deeds He worked in history for our salvation. Now our words recognize this and celebrate it. *"To you, therefore, most merciful Father, we make humble prayer and petition."*

These beautifully composed words are dense. A single phrase acknowledges before God what He has done for us. Each Eucharistic

Prayer precisely takes on a Trinitarian shape. We acknowledge to the Father what He has done for us, and then to the Son and the Holy Spirit. This is the biblical sense of confessing. We *remember* before God what He has done, and our narration lifts into the present in our midst the saving event recalled.

In Eucharistic Prayer III we sense a climax of God's plan us: *"so that from the rising of the sun to its setting a pure sacrifice may be offered to your name."* This expression echoes Malachi 1:11, which the early Christians held dear as a prophecy of the Eucharist. *"From the rising of the sun, even to its setting, my name is great among the nations; and everywhere they bring sacrifice to my name and a pure offering."* The Eucharist is our "sacrifice" and "pure offering." to the glory of His name.

THE FIRST EPICLESIS

Epiclesis in the Eucharistic prayer is the special invocation of the Holy Spirit. Literally in Greek it means *"calling down upon."*

We saw that the first movement of prayer after the Sanctus (Holy, Holy, Holy) was an acknowledgment of what God has done for us in creation and history as an unfolding of the Trinitarian mystery. There is mention of sacrifice for all that God has prepared for us and for what we are about to do. After this first movement of the prayer, there is a notable shift called the *epiclesis*. What we ask for in this moment is based on what God has shown His plan to be, that a perfect offering be made to Him.

This is the bread and wine offered by the faithful, and we dare to ask that these be changed into the Body and Blood of Christ that a pure sacrifice may be offered to His name. Here, in the gesture of epiclesis, the priest's hands are stretched out over our bread and wine, invoking that *the Holy Spirit make holy these gifts by sending down Your Spirit upon them like the dewfall, so that they may become for us the Body and Blood of our Lord Jesus Christ. (cf. Eucharistic Prayer II)*

The action of the Holy Spirit in this moment parallels the Spirit's role in the life of Jesus. When Jesus took bread and wine into His hands the night before He died, the moment and its possibilities had been long in preparation by the work of the Holy Spirit. We recall that the whole of Israel's history was destined to converge in this moment and its meaning. Hebrew Scriptures bore testimony to the Exodus which was an accomplished fact, around which the entire history centers both before and after. A memorial feast given by the Lord brought each new generation of

Israelites under its force. Jesus himself had celebrated the feast many times during the course of His life, as had His disciples. A history, a language, a vocabulary, a set of rituals gave substance for Jesus' use in that moment. He takes into His hands what the Spirit had prepared for Him; and over it all He pronounces the words that the Spirit with whom He is anointed moves Him to utter, *"This is my Body, this is my Blood."* His mission brings the history of Israel to fulfillment. What the meal shows echoes with words and gestures and food, thousands of years of history, and the very creation of the cosmos. This will culminate with Jesus' arrest, His Death, His Resurrection, His Ascension, the Pentecost of the Spirit. All this the Spirit shapes into the events that are the perfectly articulated life giving Word of the Father to sinful humanity.

INSTITUTION NARRATIVE: WORDS OF CONSECRATION

Following the epiclesis, where we see the Spirit's role so clearly, and come to what follows in the prayer, the *institution narrative*, the words of consecration.

Through the catechesis of the liturgy itself, Catholics come to understand that *Christ's sacrifice on Calvary is present at Mass*, and this reality is especially associated with the institution narrative that remembers the Last Supper on the night before Jesus died. The Last Supper pointed to the meaning of the Cross, whose meaning is finally revealed in the Resurrection and the rest of the unfolding of the Paschal Mystery. To remember the Last Supper, which by pre-figuring His Death already was swept up in its hour, is our way of remembering His Death; for the Last Supper now "re-figures" for us that hour and is thereby swept up in it.

All memorials, all liturgical remembering refers to this central event of salvation history. The risen presence of the crucified one is the eternally present fact of the new creation, the new covenant. In this sense the sacrifice of Calvary is present and re-presented in the transformed bread and wine which have become the Body and Blood of Christ.

The action, signs and symbols of this memorial mystically and mysteriously bonds us in this moment to the nexus and peak central event of human history, the salvation of the world.

Throughout all this action and the accompanying words, it remains important for us to remember with attention that it all happens with the bread and wine that we brought; for this is how our communion in the one sacrifice of Christ is accomplished. In effect, by means of our bread and wine our lives are taken up into the one and only story in which the history of the world finds its meaning and fulfillment, the Death and Resurrection of Christ. It is our lives over which Jesus' once pronounced words continue to be pronounced. And it is under these words, under this blessing, that our lives are transformed, and are allowed to become, and to declare His voluntary Death, His sacrifice.

It is good to note that the priest speaks and acts in the name of us all in our coming to the Father through Christ. The Holy Spirit shapes and supports our prayer. But even while we are moving toward the Father with our prayer, He is already coming to us, answering our prayer immediately by sending the Spirit and by sending the Son. At this point in the liturgy we are completely immersed in the mystery of the Holy Trinity and the movement of love which continuously flows among Father, Son, and Holy Spirit. The movement is in both directions at once, we toward the Father and the Father toward us.

CONSECRATION

The priest continues his intimate conversation reminding God that we make our offering in obedience to the command of His son, Jesus Christ. On the night before He died, He announced His imminent death, its purpose and the nature of the memorial His disciples were to keep of His sacrifice when he emptied himself in *kenosis*.[28] Jesus gave His disciples his body and his blood for their food. The words He used that night and his command that His actions were to be repeated in *anamnesis (remembrance)* of His sacrifice were handed on by the Apostles to their followers and also transmitted through the Epistles and Gospels.

At each Mass, the consecration takes place when the priest takes the bread in his hands, prays over the bread, and says,

---

[28] In Christian theology, kenosis (Ancient Greek:' literally 'the act of emptying'') is the 'self-emptying' of Jesus' own will and the relinquishment of divine attributes by Jesus Christ in becoming human. See scriptural reference in Phil 2: 6-7, "...he *emptied himself*, taking the form of a slave, being born in human likeness..." This action of Jesus Christ is the perfect model for Christian humility and incarnational theology. It shows the path that Jesus took from glory to degradation. It is a succinct model of a Christian spirituality: *"Let the same mind be in you that was in Christ Jesus."* (Phil. 2:5) We learn how Jesus followed his path from the glory and power of the godhead to the poorest of humble estate.

> "TAKE THIS ALL OF YOU, AND EAT OF IT, FOR THIS IS MY BODY, WHICH WILL BE GIVEN UP FOR YOU."

The priest then takes the cup of wine, prays over it, holds it up and says,

> "TAKE THIS, ALL OF YOU, FOR THIS IS THE CHALICE OF MY BLOOD, THE BLOOD OF THE NEW AND ETERNAL COVENANT, WHICH WILL BE POURED OUT FOR YOU AND FOR MANY FOR THE FORGIVENESS OF SINS. DO THIS IN MEMORY OF ME."

When the priest takes the bread and wine in his hands, he is imitating the actions that were handed down to us through an unbroken line of bishops. The words he uses as he consecrates[29] the bread and wine, the words of institution he speaks in solidarity with the Apostles who imitated Christ, these words are a combination of the words of institution written down by Paul in his First Letter to the Corinthians and recorded by Mark, Matthew and Luke in their Gospels. *"We carry out this command of the Lord by celebrating the memorial of His sacrifice. In so doing, we offer to the Father what he has himself given us: the gifts of His creation, bread and wine, which by the power of the Holy Spirit and by the words of Christ have become the body and blood of Christ. Christ is thus really and mysteriously made present." (CCC 1357)*

At the moment of the priestly action and words, an ordinary human being performs an action of extraordinary power; ordinary food becomes extraordinary sustenance. God is present in our midst, sacrificing himself to our need – food for eternal life.

---

[29] CCC 1376 The Council of Trent summarizes the Catholic faith by declaring: "Because Christ our Redeemer said that it was truly his body that He was offering under the species of bread, it has always been the conviction of the Church of God, and this holy Council now declares again, that by the consecration of the bread and wine there takes place a change of the whole substance of the bread into the substance of the body of Christ our Lord and of the whole substance of the wine into the substance of his blood. This change the holy Catholic Church has fittingly and properly called transubstantiation."

CCC 1363 In the sense of sacred Scripture, the memorial is not merely the recollection of past events but the proclamation of the mighty works wrought by God for men. In the liturgical celebration of these events, they become in a certain way present and real. This is how Israel understands its liberation from Egypt: Every time Passover is celebrated the Exodus events are made present to the memory of believers so that they may conform their lives to them.

ACCLAMATION

Following the words of consecration of the bread and wine into the body and blood of Our Lord, Jesus Christ, the priest calls the assembly to respond in acclamation to the Mystery of Faith.

Every time we celebrate the Eucharist, the work of redemption is carried out.[30] How can we rightly respond to such an incredible act of generosity? The assembly cries out with astonishment and thanksgiving. We announce our faithful adherence to the truth handed down to us from the Apostles. *"We proclaim your death, O Lord and profess your Resurrection until you come again."* We say "yes" to Jesus, which is what God asks of us.

A FEW WORDS ABOUT THE EUCHARISTIC PRAYERS[31]

The "Roman Missal," the book containing the prayers, readings and liturgical directions for Mass, has a number of Eucharistic prayers of various lengths authorized by the Church for use in praying Mass. The wording of the memorials, invocations and petitions of each prayer differs from the others, but in every one the prescribed words and memorial actions for consecration of the Eucharist are precisely the same.

THE "ROMAN MISSAL"

The *Roman Missal* is the official text of the prayers, actions and readings to be used at Mass. Each Eucharistic prayer always includes: the proclamation of the Word of God; thanksgiving to God the Father for all his benefits, above all the gift of his Son; the consecration of bread and wine; and participation in the liturgical banquet.[32] The text includes a

---

[30] CCC1364 In the New Testament, the memorial takes on new meaning. When the Church celebrates the Eucharist, she commemorates Christ's Passover and it is made present the sacrifice Christ offered once for all on the cross remains ever present." As often as the sacrifice of the cross by which 'Christ our Pasch has been sacrificed' is celebrated on the altar, the work of our redemption is carried out."

[31] CCC 1352 The "Anaphora": The Eucharistic prayer of thanksgiving and consecration is where we come to the heart and summit of the celebration.

[32] CCC 1408 The Eucharistic celebration always includes: the proclamation of the Word of God; thanksgiving to God the Father for all his benefits, above all the gift of his Son; the consecration of bread and wine; and participation in the

collection of *'General Instructions of the Roman Missal' (or simply GIRM)* for the proper rubrics and order of the liturgical celebration. The first universal and uniform missal called the *"Tridentine Missal"* was promulgated following the Council of Trent in the late 1500s. It was developed so that the whole Church would express its common identity and communion through the uniformity of its prayer and instruction. The lectionary of the *"Tridentine Missal"* was based on the Gospel according to Matthew. It remained unchanged for 400 years.

The Roman Missal was revised after the Second Vatican Council. The most significant change was a greatly expanded lectionary, that includes all four Gospels and a great amount of the Old Testament, Acts of Apostles, and Epistles in three annual cycles, A, B and C for Sundays and Holy Days and Cycle I and II for weekdays.

---

liturgical banquet.

Rev. David Rosenberg

LESSON 7

Anamnesis: Remembering our Past – Christ's Intercessions

REMEMBERING OUR PAST: MEMORIAL PRAYER, "ANAMNESIS"

The last words of Jesus, which He pronounced over the cup of wine, were, *"Do this in memory of me."* The Greek word in this text for memory is *"anamnesis."* Similar to the word epiclesis, *anamnesis* has long been used as a liturgical term to designate a part of the Eucharistic prayer. It literally means *"a memorial,"* and in the broadest sense refers to a dimension of the whole Eucharistic prayer as a narration of God's self-giving love. At the same time, it also refers to a specific part of the Eucharistic prayer following the institution narrative and acclamation: a prayer of remembrance in which the Church calls to mind the Lord's passion, resurrection and ascension into heaven. *"Therefore, O Lord, as we celebrate the memorial of the saving Passion of your Son, His wondrous Resurrection and Ascension into heaven…" (Eucharistic Prayer III)*

This part of the Eucharistic prayer also contains the second epiclesis, whereby the priest calls upon the Holy Spirit, asking not that the gifts be transformed into the body and blood of Christ but that those who receive the gifts may be transformed. This shows that the transformation of the bread and wine into the body and blood of Christ is for our sake, that we may be further incorporated into the body of Christ. The Church prays, *"Humbly we pray that, partaking of the Body and Blood of Christ, we may be gathered into one by the Holy Spirit." (Eucharistic Prayer II)* Through this mystery, the sacrifice Christ offered for our salvation to God the Father by His death on the altar of the cross remains present.[33]

OFFERING

We are reminded that the Eucharistic is not only a feast, but is also a sacrifice. *"May He make of us an eternal offering to you, so that we may obtain an in heritance with your elect" (Eucharistic Prayer III)*. The Eucharist is a sacrifice because it re-presents (makes present again) the sacrifice of the Cross and applies its fruit to the body of Christ. Therefore, the sacrifice of Christ and the sacrifice of the Eucharist are one single sacrifice.

Through this sacrifice of love, our relationship with God is restored. Christ atones for our faults and makes satisfaction for our sins to the

---

[33] CCC 1362 - 1364

Father. Christ's reconciling death brings humanity into communion with God *"through the blood of the covenant, which was poured out for many for the forgiveness of sins."*[34]

INTERCESSION OF CHRIST: PRAYING FOR OUR LOCAL CHURCH AND THE CHURCH AROUND THE WORLD

"Remember, Lord, your Church…" (*Eucharistic Prayer II*) Following the memorial prayer, the priest prayerfully proceeds to ask for the intercession of Christ for others. With our hearts now on fire, we should never fail to be moved that Christ intercedes for His Church spread throughout the world; the pope as servant of unity, the bishop who is responsible for the Eucharist in this particular Church, and the community of the faithful that down through the ages have fallen asleep.[35]

St. Monica said it well, *"Bury this body anywhere! Don't trouble yourselves about it! I simply ask you to remember me at the Lord's altar wherever you are."*[36]

The prayer opens us to the needs of the entire world by including in the intercessions those whose faith was known at their death to God alone *(Eucharistic Prayer IV)*, and all who were pleasing to Him at their passing from this life *(Eucharistic Prayer III)*.

It should astonish us as we each participate in this public prayer of the Church and the power it unleashes for the good of the world. Every single hour of every day, all the Masses prayed everywhere encircle the earth with praise and petition as they are lifted up as a gift to the living God.

THE DOXOLOGY

In ancient times, the image of the Church was often depicted as a woman in prayer with arms outstretched in the praying position. Outstretched arms remind us that Christ stretched out His arms on the cross. It is always through Him, with Him and in Him, that the Presider, representing all the Church, offers the Doxology Prayer to Christ who intercedes for all humanity:

---

[34] CCC 610

[35] CCC 1369-1371

[36] Rev. J.M.Lehen, PhD, translator, The Confessions of St. Augustine (Tolowah, NJ: Catholic Book Publishing Corp., 2013).

> *"Through Him, and with Him, and in Him, O God, almighty Father,*
> *in the unity of the Holy Spirit,*
> *all glory and honor is yours, forever and ever."*[37]

In this moment the Church is doing what Christ did and forever does: she offers His one body, to which she has been joined, to the Father for the glory of His name and for the salvation of the world. This is our communion in the sacrifice of Christ. This is perfect praise.

The Trinitarian shape of this final doxology is powerfully asserted. This is the finale of what is directed to Him. Through Him, and with Him, and in Him is the path that leads to God the Father. Throughout the prayer we are conscious that with every "through Christ" there is an "in the Holy Spirit," now in the finale we add a word to the Spirit's role, which characterizes the person of the Spirit within the divine Trinity as well as the Spirit's work in us: we say "in the unity of the Holy Spirit." We see here how praise (*doxology*) is the perfect summary for what we have remembered (*anamnesis*) and what we have asked for (*epiclesis*). This is always *the full shape of Christian prayer*.

With words and gestures the Celebrant holds up the Body and Blood of Christ, and offers these to the Father in order to give Him glory and honor. The direction of movement is clear. The whole world is coming toward the Father through Christ, and this is likewise the work of the Church. In this perfect moment of *Barakah* the Father is overwhelmed by what He sees coming toward Him. He sees His Son coming and the whole world reconciled to Him in the Body of His Son. At the Offertory the *Barakah* has been revealed to us that God the Father, in a heart-swelling love, receives the greatest gift we could possibly offer to Him, His Son, Christ. In this final Doxology of praise, we acknowledge that the Father has given His Son to the world. In His sacrifice on the Cross the Son destroys in His own body the sins of us all. Now in that same body, risen from the dead, He brings us all as one body before His Father and says, *"This is for your glory and honor!"* The Father sees His Son clothed in our flesh, in His crucified and now risen Body. In seeing His Son, He sees us, Christ's Mystical Body, as well, for there is no other Son. The Father exclaims, *"Beloved Son, in whom I am well pleased!"* The whole world is reconciled to God. This is what happens at Mass. In this moment we stand at the crossroad of our definitive future.

---

[37] CCC 1368b

The Great "Amen!"

The Presider has led this prayer, speaking in the name of the Church, acting in the person of Christ. The assembly experiences through his leadership the indispensable mediation of Christ. We have followed Christ through the memorial of His Death and Resurrection and arrive with Him in the presence of the Father. To all that Christ has done, to all that is happening, the assembly cries out a resounding Amen. *This is the most expressive and profound Amen of the Mass and world.* Throughout the liturgy we have been preparing for this Great Amen! We now have all the articles of the Creed, Father, Son, and Holy Spirit as a lived reality. This is an Amen echoing round the globe, echoing through the centuries, echoing in the halls of heaven. This Amen never ends. In the Mass, from our own place and time, we join this eternal Amen, and we shall sing forever what we are singing now. AMEN!

The Eucharist renews the Church and forges her people, the mystical body of Christ. Here, we prepare to receive the Eucharist so that we might come to be more closely united with Christ. Through the Eucharist, Christ unites us to all the faithful in one body, His Church.[38] This "communion," then, must certainly renew, strengthen and deepen our baptismal bond. If we, therefore, are Christ's body and members, then it is our own mystery that is placed on the Lord's Table. It is a priceless gift for us to receive. Realizing this, we exclaim and respond the Great "AMEN!" -- "YES, IT IS TRUE!"

At the conclusion of the Eucharistic Prayer when we say, *"Amen"* we agree that Jesus was truly, really, and substantially present with us and the only source of blessing. As we prepare for Communion, we iterate our firm belief that the peace we have offered to each other has only one source, Christ.

After the great Amen that closes the Eucharistic Prayer, the whole assembly stands because it has been carried by this prayer into the very presence of God and into its future in Christ. The congregation assembled before the altar with its priest at the center is a mystery. Joined with this assembly is the assembly standing with Christ in heaven before the throne of God. Now begins the *Communion Rite*. Love is happening here, what the ancient church called the Love Feast; Love is revealed. Love is communion. Love is Church's experience of communion in the Eucharistic celebration. Love cannot be defined by simple words or feelings or in a worldly way.

---

[38] CCC 1369

For the Christian, schooled in this moment of the liturgy, love is not like anything. Love is what is happening now.

What love is, is revealed by God here and now. As we read in 1 John 4: *"GOD IS LOVE!"* divine love is revealed here at this point in the celebration. The Church is now standing within the one love of the Father, Son, and Holy Spirit. This divine Trinitarian love, *"Cor ad cor loquitur," "heart speaking to heart,"* has a form, a shape, a dynamic; and it is all revealed in what is possible for the Church in this moment. All that follows in the Communion Rite is what is possible for the Church now.

Rev. David Rosenberg

Lesson 8

The Eucharistic Feast: Bread that is Broken and Shared

The Lord's Prayer: Our Petition for Unity

It is God the Father who has prepared this sacrificial feast as the Presider prayed the words of consecration. Christ offers His passion and sacrifice, and the baptized which constitute the Mystical Body of Christ offer their suffering and sacrifice to the Father, and all is poured into the Cup of Suffering on the altar in perfect oblation. The Holy Spirit transforms our meager gifts of *Barakah*. The Father sent the Son. The Father and the Son send the Spirit. We hear them speak with a single voice in the Liturgy of the Word. We confirm our belief in their presence and cry out loud our praise with our "Great Amen." Now we answer the implicit question of why we have such confidence in the rightness of our presence here with the Father. We are here because we are His adopted sons and daughters. At Mass, we say most appropriately the prayer Jesus gave us as we address our Heavenly Father who has loved us since our conception; together we say "Our Father…"

There is a precise reason why the Lord's Prayer is recited at this moment. Its recitation here is the foundation of our Christian prayer life. Here its original and fullest meaning is revealed and defined. In our discussion of the doxology which concluded the Eucharistic Prayer, we saw in effect that by the sacrifice of Christ we have been thrust into the very heart of the Father and thrust into our definitive future with God. The offering of Christ's sacrifice to the Father climaxes with the words of the doxology. And now the Communion Rite begins with the words *"Our Father."*

The "us" is not simply the particular assembly praying. The assembly prays in the name of the whole world that the whole world be freed from all evils, past, present, and future, that the whole world be freed from Satan, the evil one.

These are the very words that Jesus taught us to pray, and they could not be more forcefully directed to the Father than in the present moment of the Mass as we prepare to receive the Body and Blood of the Father's Son. The prayer finishes with a cry for deliverance that is at once anguished and filled with hope. In what follows, the prayer's last petition gives way to a different prayer. The priest prays alone a kind of expansion of the last petition:

"Deliver us, Lord, we pray, from every evil graciously grant peace in our days, that, by the help of your mercy, we may be always free from sin and safe from all distress as we await the blessed hope and the coming of our Savior, Jesus Christ."

Our place of prayer is a middle ground: on the one hand, the evils of this world; on the other, the coming of Christ from the future. In this middle ground the whole assembly adds *doxology* to the priest's expanded petition, a doxology which we can utter precisely because in hope we see our Savior coming. Thus, we conclude our dialogue with the Father, these words of communion with Him, by saying,

"For the kingdom, the power and the glory are yours now and forever."

THE SIGN OF PEACE

Here the priest petitions Jesus Himself:

Lord, Jesus Christ, you said to your apostles
Peace I leave you, my peace I give you.
Look not on our sins,
But on the faith of Your Church.
And grant her peace and unity
In accordance with your will
As we await the blessed hope and the coming of your kingdom.

Mass is never a private event. The "many" are always present either by intention or in the flesh. At Sunday Masses, there are brothers and sisters present to offer with Christ the sacrifice and to share the food of the cross. Just as festal meals in human families can be burdened by tension between family members and memories of unkind actions, so, too, can the Eucharist. In the Lord's Prayer, we express our hope that God will forgive us and promise our host that we will forgive others. We fulfill our promise at the "*Sign of Peace.*"[39] At the moment when we touch hands and say with conviction, *"Peace be with you"* we complete in action what was offered at the start of the Mass in the opening dialogue between Presider and assembly. We become a reconciled assembly, a sign of God's expectation for the children He created.

---

[39] CCC 1301

This Prayer for Peace is a prayer for communion between the assembly and Christ's Body and Blood that we are about to receive. The prayer recalls our Lord's words at the Last Supper in which He Himself in effect calls His Body and Blood by this other name, peace. He said, *"I leave you peace, my peace I give you" (John 14:27).* These words are part of a long discourse in which on the night before He dies Jesus explains to His apostles the meaning of the Death He is about to undergo. Explaining the same, He had said, *"This is my Body, this is my Blood."* It is good to remember in this moment that without the Lord's instruction, without divine assistance, we could not penetrate the mystery of His Death. Hidden in His Death is our peace. Thus, the first thing the risen Lord says to His apostles in appearing to them is, *"Peace to you!" (John 20:21).* As we prepare to receive His Body and Blood, we recall that peace He once promised, peace and unity in accordance with His will.

Then the priest greets the assembly with the very words of our risen Lord, *"The peace of the Lord be with you always."* The assembly answers, *"And with your spirit."* Then the priest instructs the assembly, *"Let us offer each other the sign of peace."* All the members of the assembly turn to those near them in the *"kiss of peace"* saying, *"Peace be with you,"* a gesture signifying our love for one another in Christ as we join together as one body in Christ.

We embrace one another in the peace that comes from the sacrifice offered, and at the same time we are making a sign of the reality signified in the sacrament we are about to receive. This rite has the potential for insisting to those who are to receive the Body and Blood of the Lord do so realizing that the Lord who is received unites the assembly in himself as one body.

BREAKING OF THE BREAD

One of the most ancient names by which Christians called the Mass was *"the breaking of the bread,"* a designation found in the Acts of the Apostles (Acts 2:46). There was a practical dimension to this action. It was necessary to break the host into pieces so that it could be shared among those present, but this practical action was immediately seen as a metaphor for the deeper reality that was unfolding. Saint Paul said it in a way that marked the community's consciousness ever since: *"Is not the bread we break a sharing in the body of Christ? Because the bread is one, we, many though we are, are one body, for we all partake of the one bread" (1 Corinthians 10:16-17).* Many are made one by sharing the one host; that is, the one body of Christ. With the bread being understood to be the body of Christ, it was not possible to break the bread without seeing in this ritual action an image of the Lord's Body on the cross being "broken" in order to give us life, to be distributed to us. This is already implied in the way the evangelists report the Lord's action and words at the Last Supper, summarized in the words as we use them in the institution narrative: *"... broke the bread and gave it to them, saying ... 'THIS IS MY BODY.'"* At this point of the liturgy, the priest and deacon prepare for distribution to the faithful the consecrated "bread that is broken" and the consecrated wine that is "the cup of salvation."

COMMUNION RITE

The Lamb Of God: Expressing Unworthiness And Hope

The assembly joins in singing the *Agnus Dei*, *"Lamb of God."* He is our Passover Lamb whose Body has been sacrificed, whose Blood has been poured out for the forgiveness of our sins. We acknowledge this: *"Lamb of God, you take away the sins of the world..."* and we ask Him for mercy. On the last time we ask for the even larger gift for which we have already prayed: *"Grant us peace."* This hymn is the same song sung eternally in the feast of heaven which the apostle reported in the book of Revelation: *"As my vision continued, I heard the voices of many angels who surrounded the throne and the living creatures and the elders. They were countless in number, thousands and tens of thousands, and they cried out, 'Worthy is the Lamb that was slain!'"* (Revelation 5:11-12).

Next, the sacred gifts are distributed. To begin this solemn moment the priest holds up before the people the broken bread as he says, *"Behold the Lamb of God, behold Him who takes away the sins of the world. Blessed are those called to the supper of the Lamb."* What appears as broken bread you see before you, what appears as wine poured out in your presence is nothing less than Christ himself among us come as our food, come among us in the form of the sacrifice that takes our sins away. This is the supper of the Lamb of which the book of Revelation speaks, the eternal heavenly banquet already begun, the wedding feast of the Lamb.

As the Presider and concelebrants elevate the chalice and host all the people pray together:

> *"Lord, I am not worthy that you should enter under my roof,*
> *but only say the word and my soul shall be healed."*

Saint Paul writes what is revealed as the Body of Christ. *"Now you are the body of Christ, and each one of you is a part of it. (1 Corinthians 12:27)* As the mystical Body of Christ, we are placed on the altar of sacrifice in the mystery of this great sacrament.

At this point the Communion Antiphon can be chanted, or the assembly are invited to join in singing a hymn, the words of which open up further this symbolic dimension.

In a miraculous and marvelous way, we are now One in Unity as the Mystical Body of Christ. The reception of Communion is not merely so many individual believers. It is an extension of the mystery of the Trinity as three persons in one God. In the same way we are many persons as one body united with Christ the head of this mystical body, and animated by the one Spirit who raised this body, the Church, from the dead. In this oneness that is accomplished by the reception of Communion by all and in the sign which is thus made, we can then see in the Church the sign, the image, of the Holy Trinity as many who are one. Within the Sacred Heart of Jesus we dwell within the eternal house of the Son. The name for this is love.

"Love then consists in this: not that we have loved God, but that He has loved us and has sent His Son as an offering for our sins" (1 John 4:10).

EXPRESSING OUR GRATITUDE: PRAYER AFTER COMMUNION

Be doers of the word, not hearers only![40]

Following Communion, a quietude pervades the house of prayer as each member is centered within the Sacred Heart of Jesus. *"Lord, to whom shall we go? You have the words of eternal life. We have come to believe and to know that you are the holy one of God."*[41] The Presider sits for a few quiet moments, and then all stand. He offers a final prayer, the *Prayer after Communion*,[42] and blesses the assembly. He sends forth the assembly to live out a God-given mission, uniquely crafted to fulfill God's purpose, to glorify the Lord and to be disciples of His Gospel!

The Mass ends as it began under the sign of the cross *"in the name of the Father, and of the Son, and of the Holy Spirit."* Like holy bookends, the assembly is sealed beginning to end with the love of God. The priest traces in blessing over the assembly a large sign of the cross, saying, *"May almighty God bless you, the Father, and the Son, + and the Holy Spirit."* As he does so, the

---

[40] James 1:22

[41] John 6:68-69

[42] GIRM 30

people mark again the sign on their bodies and say, *"Amen"* to the blessing.

After the blessing, the priest or the Deacon of the Word, if present, in some short phrase, dismisses the people, sending them out. It is for the baptized to be grasped within the dynamic of Jesus' words, *"As the Father has sent me, so I send you"* (John 20:21; 17:18). This expresses the Trinitarian mystery in which the Son comes forth from the Father. In that same way, from those same mysterious depths, the baptized come forth now from the risen Lord and is sent into the world. Now the assembly has been made Church, and this is the Church in the world.

In Latin, the words used for centuries for the dismissal have been *"Ite missa est,"* and from this the whole Eucharistic celebration derives one of its names, *"the Mass,"* from *"missa," "The Sending."* Missa, our mission, sends us into the world in the same way that the Son is sent. Our sending implies *a "kenosis," a "self-emptying,"* a giving it over to the Lord with our full trust in His divine providence. The Church has nothing to offer the world if she herself is not first transformed and made into the one body of Christ in whom she partakes of Trinitarian life.

"I have told you everything I have heard from my Father. It was not you who chose me, but I who chose you and appointed you to go and bear fruit, fruit that will remain." (John 15:15-16).

In this moment we prepare to offer Christ himself, the eternal Son of the Father, carried now in the flesh and in the lives of His members, poured out in self-emptying love. Through communion in the Body and Blood of Christ, the whole Church and each member become for the world what Christ is for the world: *"life-giving Spirit"* (1Corinthians 15:45). And the Church becomes this through complete self emptying. *"No one has greater love than this"* (John 15:13) and love brings healing to a world that does not yet believe.

ON THE SABBATH JESUS TOOK WITH HIM PETER, JAMES AND JOHN THE BROTHER OF JAMES, AND LED THEM UP A HIGH MOUNTAIN BY THEMSELVES. THERE HE WAS TRANSFIGURED BEFORE THEM. HIS FACE SHONE LIKE THE SUN, AND HIS CLOTHES BECAME AS WHITE AS THE LIGHT.[i]

Conclusion

A Transfiguration Experience

Throughout my faith journey, first as an Extraordinary Minister of Holy Communion at Mass, then as a deacon and now as a presiding priest, I have been privileged to witness Catholics as they receive Communion. They come to the altar, their hearts burning with desire to serve the Lord and one another; tears streaming, faces reddened, as was Moses' face, bronzed by the sight of God; people eager to go in peace, to love and serve the Lord and one another. It is my prayer that the holy Mass might become just such a transfiguration experience for you. I pray that you find a moment of Sabbath rest, where you come face to face with Jesus Christ in Word and in the Eucharist, His face shining like the sun, and His clothes radiating "as white as the light." This blessed experience is yours for the asking. Ask the Holy Spirit! He will fill your heart!

The lessons contained in this little booklet were written to be a source of inspiration to become more fully engaged in the sacrament of the Eucharist, our holy Mass. As I stated in my preface to this book, this desire rises from our Constitution on the Sacred Liturgy, *Sacrosanctum Concilium*, which so aptly states:

> *Mother Church earnestly desires that all the faithful should be led to that fully conscious and active participation in liturgical celebrations which is demanded by the very nature of the liturgy. Such participation by the Christian people as a chosen race, a royal priesthood, a holy nation, a redeemed people (1 Pt. 2:9; cf. 2:4-5), is their right and duty by reason of their baptism ... This full and active participation by all the people is the aim to be considered before all else; for it is the primary and indispensable source from which the faithful are to derive the true Christian spirit.*

Indeed, you are a chosen race, a royal priesthood, a holy nation and a redeemed people. Your full and active participation is an indispensable source of the true Christian spirit. My prayer is that today as you read this you might have David's psalm written on your heart:

> *O God, you are my God; I seek you; my soul thirsts for you. Psalm 63*

May you give thanks to the Father, through Christ, in the Holy Spirit, for all His works: creation, redemption and sanctification! May you go forth in unending praise and sing to the thrice-holy God.

Made in the USA
Middletown, DE
05 October 2022

11995341R00056